VENUS

OF KHALA-KANTI

ANGÈLE KINGUÉ

THE GRIOT PROJECT
Series Editor: Carmen Gillespie
Bucknell University

This book series, associated with the Griot Project at
Bucknell University, publishes monographs, collections of essays,
poetry, and prose exploring the aesthetics, art, history, and culture
of African America and the African diaspora.

The Griot is a central figure in many West African cultures.
Historically, the Griot had many functions, including as a community
historian, cultural critic, indigenous artist, and collective spokesperson.
Borrowing from this rich tradition, the Griot Project Book Series defines
the Griot as a metaphor for the academic and creative interdisciplinary
exploration of the arts, literatures, and cultures of African America,
Africa, and the African diaspora.

Expansive and inclusive in its appeal and significance, works in
the Griot Project Book Series will appeal to academics, artists, and
lay readers and thinkers alike.

Titles in the Series

Carmen Gillespie, ed., *Toni Morrison: Forty Years in the Clearing*

Myronn Hardy, *Catastrophic Bliss*

Angèle Kingué, *Venus of Khala-Kanti*

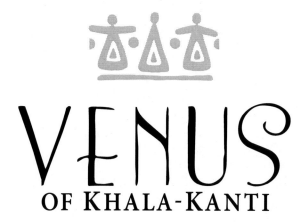

VENUS
OF KHALA-KANTI

ANGÈLE KINGUÉ

Translated by Christine Schwartz Hartley

BUCKNELL UNIVERSITY PRESS
LEWISBURG, PENNSYLVANIA

Published by Bucknell University Press
Co-published with The Rowman & Littlefield Publishing Group, Inc.
4501 Forbes Boulevard, Suite 200, Lanham, Maryland 20706
www.rowman.com

Unite A, Whitacre Mews, 26-34 Stannary Street, London SE11 4AB

British Library Cataloguing in Publication Information Available

Library of Congress Cataloging-in-Publication Data
Kingué, Angèle, 1958 – author.
    [Venus de Khalakanti. English]
    Venus of Khala-Kante / Angèle Kingué; translated by Christine Schwartz Hartley.
        pages cm. — (Griot project book series)
    Originally published in French as Venus de Khalakanti, by Ana Editions Bordeaux, 2005.
    Includes bibliographical references and index.
    ISBN 978-1-61148-628-5 (pbk. : alk. paper) — ISBN 978-1-61148-629-2 (electronic)
        1. Women—Africa—Fiction. I. Hartley, Christine Schwartz, translator. II. Title.
    III. Series: Griot Project book series.

PQ3989.2.K516V4613 2014
843.914—dc23

                                2014037513

⊖™ The paper used in this publication meets the minimum requirements of American National Standard for Information Sciences — Permanence of Paper for Printed Library Materials, ANSI/NISO Z39.48-1992.

Printed in the United States of America

To Collins, for his unwavering faith in Africa.
In memory of Ousmane Diagana, the great Peul poet,
No one sings the beauty of woman as well as you do.
And to Venus, who refuses to be forgotten....

ACKNOWLEDGMENTS

Particular thanks to Olivier Pasquet, formally of Ana Editions Bordeaux, for the first French edition of *Venus de Khalakanti* in 2005. Special thanks to Charlee Redman and Iyun Osagie for their reading of the manuscript. Warm thanks to Carmen Gillespie of the Griot Center at Bucknell University for initiating this English translation, and helping to make the story of Venus available to an English-speaking audience. Gratitude goes also to President John Bravman and Provost Mick Smyer of Bucknell University, whose timely support has helped bring this English translation to fruition. My heartfelt appreciation to Mary Elisabeth Lanser, who steadfastly refused to settle for anything but the best for Venus. Her collaboration with me in fine-tuning the translation was essential to maintaining the authenticity of the story. And finally, deepest gratitude to my heartwarmers Leanne Trout, Yannick Kingué Arienbuwa and Denise Kingué Bonnaig.

For Kari!
Read, learn & grow
Enjoy it Frieda

FOREWORD
FRIEDA EKOTTO

In Cameroon, there is a saying: "La vérité vient d'en haut, la rumeur vient d'en bas." Truth comes from political apparatchiks, while rumor comes from the marginalized. In this novel, Angèle Kingué persuades us of the reverse. She grounds the hope for a desperate African country in a remote place, the little town of Khala-Kanti, an "accidental village born of 'mislaid funds.'" It does not have viable roads, electricity, or running water. But it does have three women, Assumta, Bella, and Clarisse, who try to get by "in a world that's very capricious at times." These three women have experienced pain, and yet they do not give up; they are covered with light, despite their tragedies, and the origins of this light is the story that unfolds with the novel.

Assumta, a former sex worker, has returned from Tingui, the capital, after several misadventures related to prostitution. In Khala-Kanti she befriends Bella, a victim of cruel domestic violence on the part of her husband Boualo, a former soccer star. But Bella forgives him without resentment, while finding a space of love and compassion in Assumta's compound: women helping each other to survive the tragic. Bella helps manage the "Good Hope Center," a small restaurant-bar that Assumta opened in order to feed the truckers who find themselves in Khala-Kanti after following the road the government had paved accidentally. After Assumta passes away from complications from her HIV infection, Bella begins to work closely with her cousin, Clarisse, "the adventurer," who, two years before her return, was discovered half-dead in

Paris's Bois de Boulogne. Despite the tragedies of their pasts, it is the hope in the stories of Assumta, Bella, and Clarisse that Kingué draws from to suggest paradigmatic and poetical change. It is the source that can rejuvenate a society plagued by embezzlement, misgovernance, and the persistent failure of the so-called educated people such as Khasia, the former journalist, to understand and solve social issues.

For Kingué hope clearly has a gender; it is embodied by women. In this insight she follows Ousmane Sembène, the father of African cinema, who strongly believed Africa's freedom must begin with women. Kingué's female characters underline this belief with their strong ability for togetherness and their willingness to work with the natural world. To suggest a grounding and a power in "togetherness" is to challenge a chaotic existence. Kingué thus creates hope as a figurative space, a poetic politics that embeds a new culture in the possibility of overcoming the tragic. It is a revolt that unfolds against the assumptions that the "weak" cannot bring the transformation needed by the society. Kingué, therefore, sees in women's empowerment and in their deep sense of togetherness (*l'être-ensemble* or the "we" à la Ernst Bloch) a way to change society's soul. Bella underlines this in her reaction to those talking about her relationship with Clarisse. "We are women whose fates are intermingled, bound by a past that's heavy with impossibility and a future set with jewels made by desires and dreams. We are no longer afraid of thunder and our feet have learned to land lightly on the moss and the rocks of our forest paths." Yet Kingué understands the deep sacrifices within this transformation. Women are fundamental to the becoming of Africa, but if and only if they accept a fate in which they are "as hard and strong as a stone" in their quest for happiness. Indeed, the name Bella bequeaths upon her daughter, Mialo ma Ilali, has this very meaning.

Just as the bonds between Assumta, Bella, and Clarisse alleviate the pain of their journeys, so do their ties to the earth. They demonstrate how the forest and its trees offer hope for survival in an environment with few alternatives. Clarisse, for example, fills the trees around the Center with signs to remind their visitors of "the cult their ancestors devoted to nature, a cult they had forgotten." Clarisse connects this loss with the tragedies around her, "we have forgotten how to communicate with [nature], how to love her, how to get her to heal us. We greedily extract from her whatever we can, with arrogance, with contempt, and without gratitude. That's why we're doing so poorly in this country." But Clarisse's signs do not only remonstrate. They also allow us to sense the comfort offered in the world around them. "Let the trees support you, let your shadows intermingle," she writes. She wishes us all to be aware that we are "children of the forest."

Angèle Kingué is part of a recent generation of women writers from the continent and its diaspora (a group which also includes Chimamanda Ngozi Adichie from Nigeria, Ken Bugul from Senegal, Edwidge Danticat from Haiti, Léonora Miano from Cameroon, as well as Tsitsi Dangarembga and J. Nozipo Maraire from Zimbabwe) whose work is open to the world. These postcolonial Anglophone and Francophone authors are not writing back to the center from the periphery of Africa, but rather developing new voices that speak from and for the changing subjectivities of world citizens who live at the beginning of the twenty-first century. In Kingué's text, we hear these subjectivities singing, both through the music—the jazz—her characters listen to, and in the deeply musical prose with which she narrates their stories.

Kingué writes a new aesthetics of hope even as her attention to vulnerability makes *Venus of Khala-Kanti* a mise-en-scène of modernity par excellence. She suggests the possibilities for hope mixed together with modernity's decay. Her examination of socio-economical and political issues that put humans in danger focuses particularly upon discourses of vulnerability that language exposes, and she draws our attention to the universal difficulty of communication between people constantly searching for a decent life, for a lost country, for love and for self. Through the stories of Assumta, Bella, and Clarisse we better understand the world as it is now, in the first decades of the twenty-first century. Readers around the globe, and perhaps especially those from its social and economic margins, will be able to identify with their desire for "a future set with jewels made by desires and dreams." As bad as things are, we can take solace in being together, in loving each other, and perhaps most of all, in giving each other hope.

Frieda Ekotto is Professor of Afroamerican and African Studies and Comparative Literature at the University of Michigan. She is the author of *Race and Sex across the French Atlantic: The Color of Black in Literary, Philosophical, and Theater Discourse* (2010) as well as numerous other books and articles.

VENUS
OF KHALA-KANTI

PRELUDE

In the early morning half-light, silent shadows move with surprising precision. Clad in faded-white, short-sleeved shirts and undershirts, their green, white, and yellow wrappers are identical to the small flags they hold in their motionless hands. Marching in small groups, they approach the entrance to the village, without protest and with a silence surprising for such a large number. Blank-eyed faces, gazing mutely, sit atop moving bodies. Sunk into the deepest reaches of their souls, their eyes reveal nothing. The movements of these men and women, great-grandchildren of music made spirit, betray nothing. Nothing can be detected in them—neither fear nor anxiety, nor even indifference, to the despair of the director, nothing. It is as if, having offered up their bodies, they claimed the luxury of protecting their souls.

The director is alone in displaying feverish activity. He arrived very early in the morning, when owls are still on their last rounds. In fact, many villagers hesitated before letting him in during his rousing tour: you can never be too suspicious of night travelers. Yet, as always, out of weariness, out of habit mostly, they eventually let him in. One always lets a director inside one's home.

Khala-Kanti was accustomed to these lighters-of-the-way, these ensemble directors who poked into every last nook and cranny before some big shot's visit. But this one was after something more, he was after something better. For starters, he had not taken the village men for a traditional loosening-up drink; rather, he had set his mind on capturing the essence of Khala-Kanti, his homeland, even though it had been a very long time since he had last set foot there.

"I want to see your hearts swell and shrink, I want to hear them beat in unison," he said. "Let us welcome our dignitaries with honor and good cheer. Let us show them what the spirits of rhythm have bequeathed us." He was organizing his clapping brigade as he spoke, separating groups out on either side of the road.

"No, no, not here! There, instead. And you, you'll be here. In front of the trees. Go place yourselves in front of the trees and the *cissongo* bushes. It's you I'd like to see. I want to see some white in front of the green," he added, nervously pacing up and down the track.

What he liked best were these beautiful specimens, these fleshy men and women who allowed him to fill as much space as possible. If only he could raze this forest, which wasn't to his liking; if only he could move it so you would notice it from afar, a pretty, hazy mass, its foliage curling away forever into the distance. And what about these mud-brick houses, these spiritless abodes that didn't provide enough contrast for his set. Why hadn't he thought of whitewash—so affordable! All of the houses along the entrance to the village could have been daubed in whitewash. That would have made it so much prettier.

Caught up in his cinematic momentum, immersed in his delirium, the director could not remember his mission. The tightly packed gathering, specifically the impression of their faces so close to each other, made him feel like he wanted to do something more, "to preserve the link with his own history," he said, "to affirm his identity and trace his origins." And as if to grant his wishes, after lingering longer than usual, the moon disappeared, taking her milky light along and yielding her place to the rising sun, which set the sky ablaze. An orange light with hues of purple and blue rendered iridescent the men's and women's impassible faces, bringing to mind the tall, majestic ebony statues one hardly saw anymore except in the half-light of museums. The director was moved to tears; he couldn't have imagined a more spectacular setting. If only he could freeze this moment. If only he could make time stand still until the ministerial convoy came through. What a crowning achievement that would be for him. What a beautiful vision Khala-Kanti would become.

Before they arrived, before they could see it, visitors recognized the cheerful hubbub, the familiar buzz of market days that announced the little town of Khala-Kanti. Despite the old, canvas-covered Peugeot 404's deafening rattle, every passenger could feel the vibrations of this unexpected crossroads, this accidental village born of "mislaid funds." According to Street Radio, the only radio station in the entire region, the cessation of work on the road to the village had coincided with the less-than-graceful departure of the National Director for Road Works. He had simply been relieved from his duties, the newspapers said. But from what Street Radio was saying, he had been removed from his duties after he, himself, had removed funds from the Road Works Bureau's coffers.

And to think! This work on the road had been announced with great fanfare! Flanked by the World Bank expert, the Minister for Public Works himself had made the rounds of all the small villages in the country. There would be roads everywhere, he promised the villagers, who were lined up in their Sunday best along the edges of the road to applaud the ministerial convoy of Jeeps and Pajeros whose dust made them cough and dulled their finery. One thousand, six hundred and seventy miles of asphalt roadways were going to be expanded to a 3,106-mile highway network.

"No more dust! No more mud! Welcome asphalt! This will put an end to the agony of the pregnant woman having to struggle on foot for dozens of miles to get to the nearest hospital. This will put an end to the drama of a mother's arrival at the hospital carrying a dying child, after many long hours on the road. This will put an end to the desperation of the son clinging to his mother's lifeless body in the middle of a muddy track. And this time around, there will be no preferential treatment. There will be transparency in our decisions. Asphalt for all! Asphalt for all! We will all have it!" he concluded, caught up in the momentum of his electoral poetry.

The villagers were moved to tears. They applauded the minister. They danced in his honor. For him, they slit the throats of their goats, sheep, and roosters. From the ministerial slogans, the schoolchildren created a song they hummed as they went about:

Transparencyyyy oye,
No preferencyyyy oye,
Asphalt for all oye,
Asphalt forever oye.

The adults transmitted their enthusiasm to their children. People said: "The school walls will be less dirty." A few zealous young teachers even suggested there'd be a new school. The children, for their part, only dreamed of a less muddy schoolyard in the rainy season and a less dusty one in the dry. They were accustomed to the dust, and unfortunately, also to the spankings they received for bringing muddy clothes back home. As if the children had been able to demand that their cheap plastic sandals, known as *sans-confiance*, keep from sending mud up to their bottoms every time they took a step. The little ones couldn't make sense of it! They weren't scolded when they came home from school as dusty as farmers during the planting season, but mud seemed to exacerbate their parents' wrath. Also, for the villagers, the frequent colds and bronchitis afflicting the children were a sign of the new generation's frailty.

It would take yet another few years and, most of all, very long and complex explanations, for these dear children to understand that white is a very complicated color, a capricious color. There was the white that people knew elsewhere and then there was the white of Khala-Kanti: a dirty beige white, a white with the orange-brown hues of the dust Khala-Kanti left on everything it brushed against.

After the minister left, the people of the village dusted off their Sunday best and again donned their even dustier everyday clothes. All the villages nervously awaited the annual announcement of the new highway network locations. Khala-Kanti did not find itself on the list of the chosen few. The village mourned, along with so many other small, forgotten villages. Through Street Radio they learned that the main highway would go through a mere thirty or so miles away. "What would it cost them to extend their damn road out to us?" the old people sighed. As children of this remote corner, located at the heart of the region where the forests of the south and the savannas of the north met, the denizens of Khala-Kanti had learned to live in the oblivion that is typical of their condition. As a result, their surprise was immense when, during the one o'clock newscast, sometime later, a ministerial decree announced that the main east-west highway would make a few operational detours.

Thanks to self-centered development, Khala-Kanti found itself on the path of the country's most important main highway. This was the moment when everyone remembered Makang's appointment as Deputy Advisor to the Director for Road Works. The only son of Khala-Kanti to hold an important position in the government, this former filmmaker-turned-politician had reacted like any citizen of influence. He had abided the rule of development of the people by the people or, as Street Radio put it more simply: "It's your time to grab a piece of the cake!"

A few months later, this quiet spot, this small village of about a hundred inhabitants, turned into an impromptu garage for administration-issue tractors, excavators, chainsaws, and bulldozers looking for something to do—silent yellow machines that the country's big shots had baptized as "instruments of liberation, self-realization, and dusting off."

"How fortunate," the newly arrived teacher Khasia said. "How fortunate that these machines' yellow color goes so well with the color of our dust. At the very least, the decor remains harmonious."

Under orders to remain near their machines, the drivers were the urban planners, the architects of the newly modern Khala-Kanti. At night, they erected their tents under some mangroves, not far from the trucks. And under glorious moonlight, aided by the light of their Aïda lamps, they played ludo or checkers while drinking cases of *Ordinaire* or *33 Espéciale* beer. Every two or three days, one of the Benzes would leave for the county seat to get fresh supplies. These fleshy men also brought back supplies for the villagers, in exchange for a meal or two, and sometimes took those who wanted to go along for the ride.

Assumta befriended the big strong guy with the chainsaw. She had returned from the country's capital, Tingui, after a car accident in which she nearly lost an eye. She had been left with a large gash above her left eyebrow and a few scars on her back. During her stay in the capital, her family had announced to the village with great fanfare that she had found a job as a cashier at Printania, the big supermarket where all the expatriates stocked up.

But Street Radio, that eloquent chatterbox, informed the benevolent public that Assumta was working nights under the Banjo neighborhood's street lamps. "Doing what exactly?" Street Radio wondered with a half-smile. Perhaps expatriates only do their grocery shopping at night, it added with great bursts of laughter. Still, the news of her accident upset everyone. Say what you will about her, but this girl was generous. When she came back to the village, she forgot no one, and like a good chief's daughter, she gave more to the Street Radio members who had said the harshest things about her.

As a result, people reconsidered her friendship with the big strong guy in a positive light. What's more, the Street Radio "journalists," who also benefited from the drivers' largess, pretended not to know about this "friendship." Behind the scenes at the radio station, people merely said, and this with much affection in their voices, that the instant the big strong guy laid eyes on Assumta, he had fallen without slipping.

Assumta soon became the only person to take care of the drivers' meals. She even improvised a stand near their ludo and checker boards, from which she sold stewed game and meatballs in tomato sauce. To her surprise, her small business prospered beyond all hopes. The drivers alone ate two porcupines and two hares every night. She offered game to which these city folks were no longer accustomed. She also attributed all kinds of beneficial virtues to these meats. With great skill, she called upon these men's masculinity and virility. She was everyone's ally and mother, and above all, the big strong guy's friend.

In return for her good services, Assumta obtained the right to ride with the drivers during their supply trips to Mopoti, the small district's county seat. Every time she brought back goods that soon allowed her to open a small business.

Every day, her father, the chief, thanked the heavens for the mis-appropriation of funds that had earned his village this unexpected rest stop, this economic prosperity. He offered to build the drivers a small shed. "It'll be more comfortable than your tents. In any case, the rains are coming, there'll be water and mud everywhere, you'll be cold at night!" He had no trouble convincing them. Soon a long, rectangular building was erected and divided into several bedrooms, one for each of the six drivers. And in front of this basic building, he had a *boukarou* put up for his daughter's business.

Assumta's little establishment soon became the busiest spot in the village, to the great despair of several women whose husbands would no longer come home until the bar closed. For those whose legs were loosened by music and whose speech was revived by beer, returning home was not without incident. Money from their cocoa sales wound up in Assumta's cash register. Increasingly, evenings at the bar were regularly interrupted by the shouts of women wielding insults and even bludgeons in an effort to retrieve their husbands before all the money was gone.

You had to admit that Assumta's meat was irresistible! Some people even wondered whether she was adding a few "special ingredients" so as to attract customers. In fact, Street Radio suggested that the men fed not just on Assumta's food, but also on her charms. This revelation was broadcast during early-morning programs only, when there were few listeners around the water pipe. The news was repeated reluctantly, which was atypical for pavement radio! Listeners who were hungriest for this kind of information were offended by the suggestion.

More than once, Assumta was surprised by impromptu visits just as she was seasoning the meat. Women scrutinized every one of her gestures and tracked her every move with their intense and prying eyes, like cats waiting to pounce on fast-moving prey. Even though the women of Khala-Kanti tried hard to outdo Assumta's handiwork when cooking at home, even though they added all their Maggi cubes and *mandjangas* to their sauces, their men still slipped outside in the evening, and in secret, came to taste Assumta's *pèpèsoup*.

However, Assumta snapped sharply at boozing husbands; very frequently, she even refused to serve them. She was intent on showing the women that she wasn't responsible for their husbands' debauchery, and most importantly, that she knew how much the entire family, who had participated in working the fields, was counting on money from the harvest. In fact, women made up her largest daytime clientele; it was from her little establishment that they bought their tins of tomatoes, sardines, and mackerel, as well as their monthly bags of rice.

The first public confrontation between Assumta and the village women occurred when Narima called her a woman of the streets who was leading the entire village to perdition and swallowing up their money. After that, Assumta promised herself that no such scene would ever happen again. She went from house to house to meet with and reassure each woman in the village that she wasn't doing anything wrong and that she was just a mere shopkeeper trying to earn a living.

"Is it a bad thing that we too have our own little establishment? Is it normal that we have to go thirty-one miles every time we want to buy the least little item? So what did I do wrong for people to accuse me of causing all the troubles in this village? You all know that, like you, all I'm doing is trying to get by, and, as far as I know, I haven't killed anyone!"

Assumta began her rounds of reconciliation with six or seven women she had allowed to set up peanut and corn stalls in front of her little establishment. These women took it upon themselves to act as her defense lawyers among their girlfriends, spreading word of Assumta's good graces. Although Assumta's efforts turned out to be fruitful, her reintegration into the village continued to be difficult. Fire doesn't always put out fire, and what was needed was for the women, at least a large majority of them, not to consider her a troublemaker, an enemy, a man-eater.

She ended her conversations with a visit to the teacher, Khasia. She stayed there a long time and came out very upset. She did not utter a word to anyone regarding the nature of her visit. He was the only man she had visited. Street Radio concluded, of course, that an exchange of "energy" had taken place between them. Wasn't Khasia the village's most coveted bachelor, and wasn't it true that the big strong guy had been neglecting Assumta of late?

Even though he went regularly to the bar, especially in the evening to eat, Khasia was the strongest critic of the drivers' lifestyles—drivers who, from time to time, liked to treat the denizens of Khala-Kanti as if they were slightly dull-witted cousins. He always sat in the same corner of the bar with his tonic water and plate of *pèpèsoup*, and only looked up from his newspaper to reply to one of the drivers' quips with a sharply worded remark. Fearing that a fight might break out, Assumta tried to ease the tension by increasing the volume on the record player or asking someone an unexpected question. A good shopkeeper, Assumta tried not to upset anyone. She felt great respect and even affection for Khasia, a childhood friend, a companion in play whom she considered the only truly honest person in Khala-Kanti. He didn't mince words in saying what was on his mind, and he never took part in the malicious gossip that was spread in the village. She respected his courage. In Tingui, he'd run a gauntlet that would have annihilated more than one member of the city's elite. He had returned to Khala-Kanti not for an ephemeral visit, but to work and to reestablish himself as a member of the community. This uncommon return and his audacious loyalty had made him immune to criticism, especially by Street Radio, which for the first time in its long existence abstained from any comment.

But the drivers' feelings were also to be considered. After all, weren't they Khala-Kanti's founding fathers who consumed half of what was prepared in Assumta's kitchen? Assumta paid them the tribute their patronage deserved.

At the beginning of their stay, they had treated everyone with respect. Even though they became noisy after drinking a beer or two too many, generally people found them rather courteous and likable. They also performed numerous small favors for the people in the village. Unfortunately, their good will seemed to be dissipating. They began to raise their voices in conversation. They adopted an air of superiority and did not miss an opportunity to remind the residents of Khala-Kanti how little they knew about the world.

And then recently, the parade of girls had begun. The faces changed frequently. People saw them at night, seated around a table, smoking long cigarettes; and then also in the very early morning by the communal water pipe, drawing water to wash up. Most of them stayed for two or three days, others for weeks on end, but eventually they became bored in the small village. Very quickly they understood that the generosity of the few Khala-Kanti denizens who devoured them with their eyes was linked to the pace of the yearly cocoa harvest.

For the most part, the inhabitants of Khala-Kanti did not look favorably on this parade. But no one, not even Assumta's father, dared say anything for fear of irking the drivers, whose continued spending was the village's most substantial source of income. Several women set up their little businesses of *beignets* and beans, peanuts and other small common foods in an orbit around Assumta's little establishment. Except for the truck that came through to collect the cocoa crops, Khala-Kanti's economic life revolved around that little shop.

On a day when Khala-Kanti was napping under the burning April sun, a bus loaded with passengers stopped in front of the establishment, and changed the small village's fate. Assumta thought that an important visitor had arrived. People usually got to Khala-Kanti on foot, but from time to time small Hiace vans were willing to make the detour for an additional fee, which varied according to the state of the road. With the last rainy seasons, the road had deteriorated considerably. It had to be someone really important for a bus of this size to have braved that road. The driver got off and asked if this place was indeed owned by Assumta. She answered yes, while adjusting the braids covering her left eye.

"Well then—get out the meat, get out the bird! I've brought you some customers!"

Assumta didn't dare ask how this driver had heard of her, or how he'd convinced passengers traveling to the east of the country to make a thirty-one-mile detour to eat game. She called the women at the stands around her building to help her serve the passengers. "Smile," she told them. "Smile a lot, they'll eat more!" That night, Assumta took in her largest receipts yet. She couldn't believe it. "I hope others come." And then she had an idea. Without saying anything to the driver who had brought the crowd, she just thanked him and then, handing him a small parcel, said, "This is for your meal tonight."

Thus was born the most renowned *chantier* on the east-west highway. The little establishment, which she'd renamed "Good Hope Center," because the inhabitants were in a perpetual state of hopefulness, was now always full. In fact, she had redecorated and enlarged it. There were always one or two cars parked by the entrance. There were always clients at the bar and the pots of *pèpèsoup* were emptied at a staggering pace.

Unexpectedly one evening, to everyone's great surprise, an RV containing four German tourists traveling across Africa, off the beaten paths, stopped in front of the little establishment. Assumta gave them such a welcome that they stayed the entire night. She had two bedrooms cleaned and had the straw mattresses stuffed to give them a bit more volume. Then she made the beds herself with her best linen. Early the next day, she had basins of warm water brought for their morning wash. For breakfast, she served them stewed porcupine and plantains, which they wolfed down as though they hadn't eaten for a while. They stayed one day longer than they'd planned and talked with Assumta long into the evening. They paid her generously, promising to tell their friends, who were editing an off-road magazine, about her little establishment.

For some time now, evenings at the Good Hope Center became calmer, and Assumta, exhausted by the frequent arrival of buses, appreciated the respite. She had not even noticed that the drivers frequented the bar less and less.

While they were talking one evening just before closing, Khasia asked her, laughing, where her "guys" had gone. Before Assumta was able to respond, Pela, one of the regulars, added, "Yes, tell us. We don't see them hanging around here in the evening anymore, yet every other morning I see their trucks heading toward the track that runs along the sacred forest. On the days when I spend the night there, near my farm," he went on, "I sometimes hear them talking very late into the evening."

Khasia interjected, "I learned from one of my students that the Botta gas station is no longer accepting their gas vouchers. Ever since the work stopped, Wili, the owner, has only been paid once by the state, and he's been supplying their gas free of charge for at least six months. It doesn't look like the work is starting up again anytime soon, and Wili doesn't want to come out the loser in this. The drivers now go to Ato, the new owner of the bar across from the gas station."

"Ato is no fool," stated Dihop, whom everyone considered Street Radio's editor in chief. "Him and me, we're almost brothers. When he drinks, his tongue loosens up. The last time I stopped by his bar, he told me that he was the one supplying gas to the drivers."

"But he doesn't own a gas station," said Pokou.

Dihop burst out laughing, then added, "Look at this one here! Where is it you come from, huh? Were you born yesterday? Do you drink water in your house every day?"

"Yes," Pokou replied.

"You have running water in your house?" Dihop continued.

"No," said Pokou, looking vexed.

"Don't laugh," Dihop said to the others. "I'm only asking: he should tell us because, you never know, we may not be living in the same country." Dihop then continued with his questioning. "You have a water pipe in your house?"

"No," Pokou said again.

"Answer seriously now: you have a spring or a well in your house?"

"No," the exasperated interlocutor answered.

Dihop called the audience to witness. "I told you, didn't I? I told you he was born yesterday, this child. He's a baby bottle!"

"Hey, don't call me a baby! Me, I'm a head of household!" Pokou shot back indignantly.

"If you're no baby, why are you the only one here who believes you need to have a fountain at home to drink water? As if we were in America, where they all have Coca-Cola on tap in their houses!"

"Leave this child alone with his bad luck," someone said. "Tell us the story, Dihop."

"So I was telling you that my friend, my brother Ato, is like us all just trying to get by. You know he's only a bar owner, yet he's the one supplying gas to the drivers. He's got a buddy who supplies gas to him and who still accepts the vouchers from the Ministry for Road Works. This buddy knows someone who's well placed," Dihop continued with a knowing wink.

"We got it: Ato's buddy has a long arm."

"Exactly," Dihop concurred, adding, "Ato sells the gas back to the drivers at a higher price, almost double. Since no one else accepts their vouchers anymore, they don't balk too much. Ato pays his friend the regular price and keeps the other gas vouchers for himself."

"But he doesn't have a car," the person everyone was now calling the child exclaimed.

"Can someone bang this child on the head or else tie up his mouth, since he doesn't know how to use it?" Dihop retorted with a false air of annoyance.

Pela looked at Pokou with exasperation, and most of all despair, at his friend's extreme naiveté, for Pokou, in a little pirogue, was battling the swollen river that the world around him had become.

"What on earth is wrong with you?" he asked him.

Then, turning to Dihop, he continued, "Don't say anything. I really don't know what to do here myself, his case is too serious, leave him alone. Go on with the story for us."

Dihop resumed his explanation. "With the other vouchers, Ato buys gas that he sells in jerry cans from his house, mostly at night, and of course a little cheaper than what the gas station owner across the road charges. So guess where the customers are going now?" he asked, laughing with gleaming eyes. "People in this country may be flat on their stomachs, but they're not dead." Dihop had relished every moment of his story, as if he'd been the one who had succeeded in gaming the system.

"But if he's caught, it's prison," Pela noted.

"Absolutely not. They can't send him to prison. He hasn't done anything. You know what he told me when I asked him what he would do if things turned sour? He told me: 'This thing came to find me at my place. It came to find me in my home. I did not travel to a government office to get gas vouchers. I'm just a simple village dweller, I don't even know where the ministries are located in this country.'" Then Dihop concluded with a great burst of laughter, "And that's not all! Don't forget that the drivers let him use one of the trucks once a week so that he can buy supplies for his bar. No one's a fool!"

"Ato is really very smart. There's a great guy," exclaimed Pela, with much admiration.

"You keep on sleeping! Don't see him as you see him now. A small guy can be a big guy too. If he'd finished his studies, he'd be somebody today. But just as he is now, he could teach our big shots how to negotiate with the people who are emptying out this country," concluded Dihop, who had donned the mantle of Street Radio's designated editor.

"But if the drivers' gas vouchers are no longer accepted, it's because they're no longer being paid, their salaries must have stopped, I'm sure of it," said Pela. "Assumta, come tell us what's happening. What's the big strong guy telling you? I see them eating and drinking at the same rate when they're here!"

"Could be that our sister's financing," someone tossed out ironically. "Whereas we, her brothers, are dying of starvation."

"Don't start with me, this really isn't funny at all," replied Assumta. "I've been seeing very little of him lately. He told me recently that his wife was sick."

"Dihop, you have to look into this story," said Pela. "These drivers must be plotting something shady."

The discussion continued until late. Assumta had fallen asleep in her wicker armchair. Khasia tapped her lightly on the shoulder to pay his bill. Assumta's golden rule was to never chase her customers away. When she was completely exhausted, her father or the big strong guy would ask the last clients who were dozing between drinks to leave.

"Everyone's gone," whispered Khasia, "you can close shop."

"Thank you," Assumta replied, her eyes blinking. "I'll have to hire someone to help me. At this rate, I'm going to age before my time. Even the young ones who often come to lend a hand are sleeping already! In any case, I can't leave anyone at the cash register: everyone helps themselves as if it were the state's coffers!"

"I'll help you get the tables back inside."

With a wide, grateful smile, Assumta replied, "I always thought you hated me."

"And that would be the reason why I come here to eat your *pèpèsoup* every night?" he retorted.

"If another woman cooked, I know you'd go to her place."

"I may resent you a little for emptying out my 'school under the tree' just as I was really beginning to convince the farmers that a one-hour lesson at night would do them some good! But, if they won't come to me, then I'll simply come to them."

"Do whatever you want, but don't chase the customers away. You are worse than a priest!" Assumta lectured, half-laughing, half-serious.

"You find it normal that Khala-Kanti is mostly known for the girls the drivers drag here, huh? Do you even know that the drivers leave their rooms to other people who take the girls in there?"

Assumta's eyes opened wide. "The morons! Oh my God! What are people going to say now?"

"All this is taking place under your nose and you mean to tell me you don't know about it? You've created a brothel, my dear," said Khasia tartly.

"I swear to you on what is left of my honor that I didn't know they were passing their rooms on to other people. Sure, some drivers who come with their buses do disappear for an hour or two, but me, I'm serving the customers and staying by the cash register, I couldn't guess what they were doing. You're not going to ask me to control the lives of adult men or govern their actions! I'm not going to forbid them from bringing women into their rooms!"

"Except that the women change every week, and the school isn't far from here. That's real nice for the children who come to your place to buy candy and *beignets* during recess!"

Assumta had been kept so busy building up her small commerce that she hadn't noticed the central role her little establishment had assumed in the village, much less the presence of the oldest profession in the world on her grounds.

"Khasia, you know what I lived through in Tingui. I don't wish my experiences on any other little girl in this village. Look at me. Look at this gash over my eye. Do you really think I don't have a heart?" she asked. "I want to build a big shop here, and I'm just beginning to believe that I'll be able to succeed in doing so. Ever since the buses started bringing passengers to me, the receipts have been really good. All I need is to take time to get organized."

Then after a short pause, she added, "I'd like to build a small hotel here. Since my brother Mambeti's death, my father's cocoa farm has fallen into decay. I'd like to build *boukarous* that would serve as hostels and a big shop, with the Good Hope Center next to it. That's what I'd like to do. I'd like for Khala-Kanti to become a city someday; I'd also like for our people to be able to work right here. I'd like for us to not always have to leave the village to find work elsewhere. I'd like for the village to have street lamps, and for our little girls to stop thinking that they are Christmas trees. That's my dream," she announced, her eyes shining.

Khasia didn't say anything. He was looking at Assumta intently, as if seeing her for the first time. Even her face had lost the jovial air it always displayed.

"You think I'm a madwoman?"

"Why are you saying that?" asked Khasia playfully.

"Because you're not saying anything and you're staring at me."

"That's because I'm listening to you and also, it's true, you're surprising me!"

"Ah really! And how am I surprising you? You think I'm dreaming?"

"No, no, you're not dreaming, and anyway, all new things begin with a dream, you know! No, it's just that I didn't imagine you as having lots of plans. I thought you were an opportunity queen, a good-deal specialist."

"You know," Assumta continued, "when the Germans stayed the night last month, they told me that if their friends came through the area, they would recommend Good Hope Center to them. And one of the women with them, the one who wanted to know lots of things about my use of herbs and plants, she told me my little establishment was like a good country inn. Since that time, I think about it every night, and every night I dream about it. Don't laugh," she went on, after perceiving wry amusement in Khasia's eyes. "Every night I dream that I am waking up in a soft bed, in a pretty little bedroom with flowered curtains!"

"So the big strong guy's small attentions aren't responsible for making you look so well-fed these days?" said Khasia teasingly.

"I know what you're thinking, I can see you coming from a mile away: once again you're going to tell me that money and men are all that count for me. You won't ever understand, Khasia, you won't ever understand what it's like to be lying down, on your knees, turned inside out, squatting, destitute, violated. You won't ever know what it's like to bear the weight of a man. You don't know how much a frustrated man weighs, or an unhappy man, or a violent man, or a drunken man, or a cuckold, or a plain old scumbag of a man. Me, I have inhaled the breath of all the men of this world. I have inhaled all the sordid and putrid breath of this country. I want my own bed, a bed made of clouds with a beautiful bolster made out of rainbow. As for my bedroom ceiling, I swear to you that it will be a piece of blue sky. My grandmother used to say that the dreams of the poor taste better than those of the rich. My dreams have the intensity of a woman worth nothing, but I assure you, I know where I'm going."

Lowering her voice, she whispered, "You know that the big strong guy hasn't been coming to see me for a while?"

"Yes, I heard that."

"But there's something more serious. Fortunately, Street Radio hasn't heard about it yet. My father is gravely ill and the family says that it's a curse because he sold the trees of the sacred forest to the drivers."

"So this is what their new business is, huh? As for your father, what an idea to sell these trees to the drivers!"

"No, that's not exactly it. A month ago, the big strong guy asked if I could find him a good little forest about ten miles away from Khala-Kanti, because he wanted to build a small storehouse to hold the cocoa that he had been buying from all the small villages around. He explained to me that they had yet to receive instructions from the Ministry for Road Works and that he and his colleagues had decided to make do, meaning take measures in case they stopped being paid. That's why the drivers were crisscrossing the villages to buy cocoa from the farmers at a modest price, so as to sell it to the big companies in Tingui. He successfully convinced the farmers that the cooperative would no longer make collections, and to top it all off, he told them that it was incumbent on them to bring the cocoa to the location he was giving them."

"But wait, what are you telling me? They do have co-op members' cards, and in principle, the drivers who are making the collection must also show the farmers their cards. They're used to seeing the co-op truck show up right where they live to get the cocoa bags, aren't they? Come on, really!" Khasia exclaimed indignantly.

"I've only just learned about their scheme," Assumta replied, looking aggrieved.

"See," Khasia said, "this is why my 'school under the tree' night classes mean a lot to me, so people don't swallow whole everything these imbeciles tell them!"

"In short," Assumta replied, "I convinced my father to give them a plot of land in the Bekon Forest—you know, the one where we hold the *Ndjé* ceremony and where new chiefs are consecrated. It's six miles from here—very few people are allowed to go in. But the drivers have done so much for the village that I thought they needed a safe place to hide their operation. That's why I insisted with my father, and since he trusts me, he let me go ahead. But the terrible thing is that the drivers didn't build the storehouse and instead cut all of this small forest's beautiful trees—they razed everything!"

"You asked them for an explanation?"

"Of course. The big strong guy told me they were clearing out the forest to build the storehouse, but he was ill at ease, he didn't look me in the eye."

"How did you find out what was happening?"

"You remember Lemba, my father's brother, the healer? The one whose place we went to to steal mangoes when we were small?"

Khasia smiled and nodded yes.

"He was going to look for bark in the sacred forest and fainted when he saw this massacre. It was his children who brought him back to the village. He immediately sent for my father, and there you have it."

"And how is this all connected to your father's illness?" Khasia continued.

"You've forgotten? Sometimes I wonder if you were born in this village! The other elders are accusing him of being the drivers' accomplice. After all, didn't he build a shed for them? The elders are accusing my father not just of violating the site of all the rites of the inhabitants of Khala-Kanti, but also of pocketing the money without meaning to share it. This is making my father sick, he's wasting away in plain sight, and personally I don't know what to do! No words are strong enough to describe what these bastards have done to the Bekon Forest."

"So you went there!" exclaimed Khasia, both incredulous and curious.

"I know I don't have the right to do so, but I went there anyway, without anybody knowing—or at least I hope," Assumta whispered, looking worried. "After my visit I went to see the big strong guy. I called him all kinds of names. He told me that without him we'd be nothing. It's since that time that he's been coming less and less," she sighed, adding, "The family has agreed not to say anything. I will submit to their decision. I think we'll need to hold a lot of atonement ceremonies. I know I will need to part with a good amount of money in order to calm them down."

"But why didn't you say anything? Who are you protecting?" asked Khasia.

"I wanted them to leave of their own accord, I wanted them to take their bad luck away with them! I didn't want them to take advantage of our altercation to destroy what I have built, however small it may be. That's why I didn't say anything."

"You're protecting your money, your little business, that's what it is, isn't it?"

"You don't understand anything, nothing, absolutely nothing at all!" Assumta yelled, sickened. "You haven't understood a thing of what I've been trying to tell you; you're like all the others!"

Assumta glared at Khasia.

"Why do you have your nose in here every night if you find it so disgusting? What are you doing here if this little place represents nothing? You think they'll come and build you an entertainment center, your friends from the capital? They couldn't care less about remote corners like these, they wipe their butts with them!"

Then, catching her breath, she added, "You can go to hell, you and your little school. What are your graduates becoming, what are they becoming, huh? Congrats! This gentleman here is training the capital's future little beggars. And tell me, Khasia, you big squawker, what are you hiding? What are you protecting? What's a guy like you doing in Khala-Kanti?"

Khasia's gaze had hardened. His entire body had stiffened. He pushed back the empty plate in front of him, opened his mouth to say something, thought better of it, pulled out a 500-franc note that he deposited on the counter, and headed toward the door. Assumta ran after him to beg him not to go.

"Please stay, don't go. I'm sorry. Forgive me, I know I've touched a nerve, but I'm talking to you as you're talking to me, Khasia. Stay with me tonight," she begged, pressing herself against him.

Khasia held her hand for a long while, kissed her hair tenderly, and said, "I'm not upset, Assumta. You have a right to say whatever you want. You look tired, and so am I, in fact. Rest. We will see things more clearly tomorrow."

After Khasia left, closing the door, Assumta collapsed on her bed with her clothes on. She was so tired that she didn't even have the energy to blame herself for the argument. "He's just a child," she told herself. "What took hold of me? Why do I try to solve everything with my body?" she wondered as she curled up. And her thoughts took her back to the evenings of her childhood. Evenings when adults, very serious-looking, held long, private discussions, and women kept children away as if something disturbing was in the works.

And one evening, the entire village would witness an endless parade of baskets and basins full of yams, cassava, plantains, and cocoa beans—in short, everything that was grown in Khala-Kanti's fields. The men filled their gourds with their best palm wine, and thus a festive meal, a veritable feast, was prepared for the spirits of the forest. Just before the planting began, they implored nature for her leniency. Most importantly, the union between the forest and its inhabitants, a union sanctified by the gods from time immemorial, was celebrated. Assumta's father, the guardian of the masks and the keeper of the ancestors' spirits, was the first to leave for the forest in order to speak with the genies, the masters of the place, and announce the visitors' forthcoming arrival.

Sated, satisfied with the generosity of its inhabitants, the forest in turn sent masked beings over to him, the only beings capable of deciphering her complex language, the only ones who could remind the members of the community of the incomparable virtues of the forest's trees. Each of these enchanted beings would announce his arrival with a sound that was his own. Their clothes were made of plant fiber and their drums were born from the trees for which they were the spokespersons, the symbol. Through its appearance and resonance, each tree thus entered into intimate communication with the inhabitants of Khala-Kanti. Later, when the masked beings were all gathered in a circle at the center of the village, they launched into a mesmerizing and melodious concert that evoked, in turn, the rumble of thunder, the crackling of fire in the woods, the roar of big cats, the rhythm of hoes digging the soil, and even the tinkling of rain on tin roofs. They were faithful interpreters of all the rhythms buried in the village's innermost depths.

In her mind's eye, Assumta saw once again the faces of the other children who were seated, huddled against their mothers. On these childish faces the same animation, the same sense of wonder, the same fear, could be read. Once again she saw the face of Clarisse, her cousin on her mother's side, a little city girl whose audacity always surprised her. Here she was, quivering with impatience, ready to plunge into the celebration with gusto. She'd even managed to edge her way among the men who were in the first rows.

Contrary to the other little ones, she absorbed everything that was going on around her with keen attention, with excitement, her eyes shining, her small hands moving to the sound of the drums. She would have joined the masked beings had a vigorous arm not held her back. She surprised several adults with her sense of rhythm. She moved like them, she danced with them, as if she already possessed secrets she wanted to convey to the earth. Once again Assumta saw Khasia's little-boy face; all of seven years old, he was drinking up the music that the sacred beings were extracting from their magical boxes, captivating music that he had never heard before and that resembled a heavenly chorus. One could hear nature unleashing, and then calming. Sound faded, became distant, and returned. Then a silence invaded the night, and just as these musicians of the invisible seemed to have withdrawn, the roar of the drums became louder, mixing with their heartbeats. And all the people in the village, children, women, men—all of them started to dance. Not a dance of joy and levity, as is customary in times of celebration, but a dance that was understated, slow, questioning, revealing.

They danced like a fiancée's seduction, like a lover responding to her beloved's pressing calls. First with a barely perceptible movement of the hips, small gyrations with which they drew the circle of life as if they were warming up this mankind-bearing part of the body, then stomping the ground to the rhythm of the drums, which had already espoused that of their hearts. And the earth could be heard waking up under hundreds of steps pressed against her. She could be heard moaning, whispering, tensing, giving herself, offering herself, abandoning herself to the rhythmic caresses of desire from time immemorial. In unison, in a collective jolt, these men and women no one in the world knew, this small, obscure people, in a majestic dance, with a nocturnal ballet, responded to the call of the spirits of the forest.

Later in the night, these masked beings, robed in the adornment of the forest, performed an elaborate dance along a route that led to the abodes of the afflicted, and the forest continued to lavish care on the inhabitants. At dawn, the masked beings headed back to the forest, followed by a grateful clamoring from the entire village. Assumta did not understand what was happening; her mother only told her that the harvest would be good that year, told her that many of the uncles had received good treatments for their diseases and that they would soon be better, and most important, that the harmony of hearts and bodies had been confirmed. Assumta and her little playmates were transfigured. Each year she awaited this event with impatience and the forest had never left her, even if the planting ritual was rarely practiced in the village anymore.

That night, Assumta remained awake for a long time. She felt badly about the harsh words she had had for Khasia. She knew he had forced himself to come back to the village, to accept work as a school teacher—he who had been the mouth of the entire country, an image of the word made action, as people in Khala-Kanti put it when they described the television news host. Khasia told anyone who would listen that he was fine and that he'd returned to the village because it needed people like him. He told anyone who would listen that someone had to take the first step.

Assumta knew that Khasia's nights were filled with doubts, questions, and regrets. She knew he sometimes blamed himself for not having played the game, for not acting like everyone else did. She thought back to her own first nights after her return to Khala-Kanti, nights of solitude, nights when she wondered if she might be better off leaving the village and resuming her position under the street lamps of Tingui's avenues. She wanted to get up to go see Khasia, explain that she knew what he was feeling, tell him that she knew they'd both survive. But she hesitated. She hesitated because while they'd shared the same childhood, while they'd frequented the same small school in Khala-Kanti, Assumta sometimes perceived in Khasia, not a form of contempt, but a lack of understanding for some of the choices she had made in her life. Even though Khasia had never said anything directly, she often felt his reproachful gaze upon her.

It was several weeks since the drivers had last been seen in Khala-Kanti. Assumta sometimes looked worried. The Zovatel machines were parked a few yards away from her little establishment and served as a constant reminder of the happy moments she'd spent with the big strong guy. Whatever his behavior, whatever his treason may have been, she admitted that he had treated her more kindly than all the men she had known in Tingui. That was precisely why his departure hurt. Assumta, the tough one, she who had promised herself that she would never again reveal herself, had gone soft.

For a brief instant, she believed that illusory happiness. Yet, at the same time, she refused to bemoan her lot. She ate her fill, took care of her family, fed a few destitute cousins and friends, and most importantly, felt respected. Her past on the capital's sidewalks seemed quite distant, and even Street Radio had stopped broadcasting spicy reports about her life. Everything now seemed to revolve around the Good Hope Center. Absorbed in the whirlwind of her little business's success, she launched into her commerce with the savvy and energy of a *buy-am sell-am*. Small shivers of satisfaction ran through her body as she totaled up her receipts every night.

Even if money meant a lot to her, it was the new freedom that this money provided that pleased her. "You know," she told Khasia one night, "I'm the boss of my body, of my ass. I'm the one telling it when and where to squat or lie down. It's intoxicating, it's strong, let me tell you."

At the same time, Khala-Kanti's reputation kept on growing. New vehicles were beginning to venture to the village regularly. Since Assumta had instituted a commission system with the drivers, several trucks coming from the east made the long detour to allow their clients to discover Khala-Kanti's succulent *pèpèsoup*.

Assumta enlarged her restaurant. The Good Hope Center was beginning to look imposing. The property was surrounded by a hedge of giant fichus and hibiscus plants that helped keep the dust away. Small, gravel-covered paths led to several *boukarous* cleverly located on either side of the bar. The small establishment her father had built for her had been renovated. She added large windows and light perpetually bathed the rooms. In the evening, a light breeze made the white poplin curtains ripple. She whitewashed the whole place regularly, thus making the group of buildings look neat, clean, and pretty. To Khasia, who frequently teased her about her futile battle against the dust, she replied that everyone fights his battle the way he chooses. "Others go to war with humans. Me, I'm fighting small, reddish particles. It is because my place is less depressing that people come here. They're fleeing their dusty daily life."

The drivers' little bedrooms had been improved as well. There, Assumta put small, basic beds and wicker furniture. Bedding was available for the length of stay. Occasionally, customers spent the night. But since she'd raised her prices, the majority of her hotel clientele was made up of bureaucrats from Tingui who purportedly came to spend a quiet weekend with their wives. In actuality, most of them relocated their "second offices" for the freedom to engage in love affairs. In Khala-Kanti they were more likely to elude their suspicious spouses. Even the most tenacious, the most vigilant among them, would never consider looking for their husbands in the small village.

As this practice moved from occasional to the norm, Khasia did not spare Assumta his usual sarcasm. "So now you're going big! You got this one right, going from a brothel for small fish to a brothel for big fish!"

"You're pissing me off, Khasia, you're really pissing me off! Your shit is beginning to run over the pot! Go solve your problems elsewhere, go solve the problems that made you flee the capital instead of coming here to hound me. Go fight your moralizing battle in Tingui."

Assumta glared at Khasia, the veins in her neck and forehead swollen, the words coming out of her mouth scathing, biting, as she spat out all the words she had long restrained herself from firing at him.

"Stop acting as if you were doing us the favor of living among us. No one here is responsible for what happened to you. I do my best, but look me in the eye and tell me who the clientele is over here. I'm not in the big city and businessmen aren't clamoring to get in. Neither are tourists, by the way. Once, only once, did German tourists come through. You witnessed it yourself! Would you have me travel out to bring them in? I raised my prices, and I make every effort to keep this place very clean so it doesn't feel sordid. What people do in their bedrooms is their business!"

Usually quick to respond, Khasia left the bar without a word, slightly bent over, like someone who had just aged very rapidly. Never had anyone hurled at him the truths that Assumta had just thrown in his face. Ever since his return to the village, everyone had carefully avoided talking about his life in the capital. For the most part, people were rather happy that an illustrious journalist, a great national reporter, had chosen to live among them rather than stay in Tingui. He wore his return to the fold like a badge of honor. He'd convinced himself that this was what he'd always wished for deep inside himself, and that he was being more useful to the children of Khala-Kanti now that he lived among them. In his view, his transfer home had merely allowed him to demonstrate the courage of his actions.

When he reached his house, he lay down on his bed and cried his heart out, he cried like he did the day he lost his mother. He cried out of frustration, because a woman, a former prostitute for that matter, had removed his mask. A mask he'd put on when he'd been relieved from his duties and that he wore with pride for the benefit of the capital's smart set, especially those very people who once invited him to all the functions and now pretended they didn't recognize him. But he cried mostly because Assumta had just revealed to him that he who thought himself strong, combative, rigorous, he who'd dared say "no" to the position he'd been offered, who'd preferred leaving with dignity rather than cowering before the powers that be, he,

Khasia the brave, was just a weakling, a fly, a *moumou*!

He hadn't protested, he accepted the ministry's decision with the fatalism of all those who were brought up in this country and whose combative verve had been annihilated by the system. He accepted because he knew his rebellion would come at too high a price. He could have chosen exile, as several of his compatriots had, but he couldn't find the courage to leave the country that possessed him entirely. He was convinced he would have withered like a leaf cut off from its roots.

He hadn't found the courage to leave his daily life, a daily life that, although brutal at times, fulfilled and restored him. In his view, the exile that would have guaranteed his personal freedom wouldn't have helped advance his community's causes. Still, he often wondered what the two years he'd just spent in the village had changed in his young students' daily lives. What have I contributed? Who have I influenced? Had I accepted the reporter position Joe had found for me at the *African Tribune* in Washington, D.C., I would have at least, with complete peace of mind, experienced the joy of denouncing the ills that are undermining our society.

"But why leave? Why should I be fleeing?" he asked himself constantly, tears in his eyes. For him, going into exile was tantamount to fleeing, but he was crying mostly because he had just now come to understand that one could experience exile at home. If only he were capable of acquiring the detached nonchalance that could be read on the faces around him, if only he were capable of sliding into torpor, of donning the protective shell that seemed to ensure survival. In his self-flagellation, Khasia was forgetting all the young people who, thanks to him, had obtained the first diplomas of their lives. He was forgetting his students from the "school under the tree," he was forgetting the men and women who came to see him at his place in the evening, children on their backs and chalkboards in hand. He was forgetting the joy Trécia felt when, at thirty, she was finally able to write her name.

Khasia remembered the joy he felt when he passed the entrance exam to journalism school. He could already imagine himself solving his country's problems. He could already see himself, armed with lexical arrows, dismantling the power of the various clans that had a stranglehold on the country's resources. Above all, he knew he would do better than all the others who, although armed with education, had abdicated their responsibilities. In journalism school, his favorite class was about ethics and law. His last paper, an editorial about the freedom of the press and development, had been published in the school newspaper. In it, he invoked the ways in which freedom of expression had benefited the first American colonies. In his lyrical conclusion, he wrote: "If others have done it, we Africans for whom the word is foremost, for whom freedom is the only path to the future, we have the duty to express ourselves freely as well. On this condition only shall we be able to straighten a backbone bent under centuries of servitude; on this condition only shall we rise from our daily quagmire."

Khasia was eager for classes to focus more on local politics, but the bulk of their discussions very often revolved around the study of Western democracies. From time to time, the professor touched on Latin America and the Caribbean, Cuba mostly, and he always promised to tackle Africa specifically, in future classes. When Khasia graduated as class valedictorian, he was immediately offered the position of newsreader for the new national television's 8 p.m. broadcast. The whole of Khala-Kanti was delirious with joy even though there was no reception there; the whole country knew that their most important journalist was the son of a small, insignificant village called Khala-Kanti.

From his first days, the director of United Media had informed Khasia that he wanted to see the headlines of his newscast at 7 p.m. every evening. Sometimes his folder came back with one or two headlines amputated, and in the margin, a simple note saying "delicate," "follow up," or, occasionally, the comment "wait for further instructions," which never came, especially when the subject had to do with local politics. While upset by the actions of his director, Khasia attributed this censorship to the novelty that television represented in his country and to his boss's excessive zeal.

In journalism school, none of the professors had broached the question of censorship. Mr. Bila, his old rhetoric professor, often talked about delicate news, about how it was necessary to adapt to the journalistic climate of one's country. He spoke at length about the virtues of linguistic subtlety, and most of all, about the ability to tell, to denounce, to expose, even, but without exposing oneself. His was the class that posed the most problems for students, the infamous rhetoric class, appreciated by a few but loathed by the great majority. "He wants to show us how well he masters French," the irate students said. Everybody called Bila a bitter old man who had failed to evolve with the times.

Nevertheless, old Bila reminded students that his class was the most important one in the curriculum: "I am training you for your survival," he told them. "I am teaching you how to be good journalists in the tropics. If your wish is to become two-bit *griots*, be my guests. You'll write well, you'll speak well, you'll know everything about foreign affairs and even your country's affairs, but you won't survive until you understand what I am trying to get into your heads. With your analyses and your reports, you must all at once inform your audience, alleviate your compatriots' misfortune, and ensure your own survival."

Every class was given the same speech. Many viewed old Bila as an eccentric, a driveling fool, but he was kept around out of habit, because his mastery of language was stunning, and perhaps above all because, even though he was a bother, no one had much of an idea of what they should accuse him. Just like the hare, the turtle, and all fine hounds in the forest, he survived thanks to his instinct for the danger around him. He used words with skill, redefining them as the moment dictated. He always managed to convince the media police that he'd said the opposite of what he was accused of saying. He illustrated his point with numerous examples, quotations in Latin, proverbs in Baélé, his mother tongue, and he played a thousand linguistic tricks on those who accused him of inciting revolt.

Khasia had been put on the index several times for disregarding the "temporary restrictions" his director recommended. He'd recently been suspended from the air for a month. But the public had protested and a great number had laid siege to the United Media offices. The director had been obliged to call Khasia back, informing him that there'd be no reprieve next time around. After one year at the 8 p.m. newscast and numerous petty annoyances, Khasia eventually understood what his old professor meant. He even intended to see him so as to tell him, but he was told that old Bila had died of cirrhosis a few months earlier.

Khasia thought back to his classes, to the endless discussions about the manner in which phrases were to be turned. He remembered the old journalist's golden rule: live in the conditional mode; this will be your operational mode, your survival mode. "Whatever the circumstances, all words uttered by the reporter must be in the mode of uncertainty."

"Whatever your certainties, all political comments must be expressed in the passive voice. You will use it abundantly and thus have the opportunity to allude to events that you would have otherwise had to avoid. Master the rules of the linguistic mishap. Systematically wrap every one of your critiques, especially the harshest, inside a laudatory sentence. Even when there is no other choice, you can avoid becoming a mere flatterer by getting others to speak. Interview people who are prepared to speak in your place, there are always takers; it is television. But retain whatever little dignity you have left. You owe it to your audience.

"Favor the words manhandle to brutalize, disappearance or flight of funds to embezzlement; economic conjuncture to economic crisis; slowed evolution to complete stop; outdated practices to charlatanism and maraboutism; hesitation, or better, phase of reflection to waffling or inertia." Everything came back to him in a jumble, especially the old man's favorite saying: "You can't measure a river with your two feet." He finally understood the words that everyone found exaggerated at the time.

After a year of frequent confrontations and barely veiled threats, Khasia eventually decided to become a good journalist. For the national daily, he wrote editorials that would have earned him his old teacher's congratulations, and then, as if to pay him tribute, at the end of the newscast he created a short comment about the use of the French language by the man in the street. His short program, which he first called "French in the Tropics," then "Francotropics," soon became the most watched half-hour on television. Every time the program began, Khasia would remind people that, as a good journalist, he was merely taking the nation's pulse. He was conveying the ideas and comments of the ethno-linguist, that is, every man on the street. The public outrage caused by each of Khasia's suspensions was therefore easy to understand.

The program recounted the adventures of Dieuleveu, a good citizen of the capital. In the latest broadcast, for instance, Khasia had asked him how he was doing:

"My brother," Dieuleveu answered, "We dey here o, wetin we go do now?"

"And what about work?" asked Khasia.

"What work?" Dieuleveu answered. "Haven't you heard about downsizing, retrenchment? Compression? I was compressed! Yes, my brother, I've been compressed just like they do in the hospital, with a bandage on top even, like a mummy. As you see me so, I can't even move. My wife Mado cried so hard, the entire neighborhood showed up at my house; people thought I was dead."

"But what are you going to do now?" Khasia continued.

"Hmm! I'm going to manage, like everyone out there. Wetin I see I do o; wetin I no see, I no do o. I don't want people to come mourn me again when I'm still alive."

"Good luck, Mr. Dieuleveu," Khasia concluded.

Dieuleveu burst out laughing.

"No one told you, Mr. Khasia? Luck has gone abroad. She doesn't live here among us anymore—too many mouths to feed, too many cousins and too many uncles. People were praying too much, and above all the roads were in too bad a shape. She got tired and she, too, left with the funding agencies."

The entire country followed these last five minutes of the broadcast passionately. The audience recognized its daily life in the travails of these people of the shadows. Khasia had made himself the spokesperson for the voiceless, and in the streets of the city's various neighborhoods, he became the savior-hero, the man of hope, of deliverance. So it was easy to understand why Khasia annoyed some people and why he was accused of lacking in deference.

His director had led him to understand that his intentions were opaque. He explained to a stunned Khasia that his attitude denoted a certain irreverence, a lack of admiration for the appropriate persons, a little like a child who doesn't know to lower his eyes at the right time in a confrontation with an adult.

"You should be happy you're not being sent to prison for slandering and spreading false news," the director concluded while avoiding looking Khasia in the eye. The next day, Khasia learned that he was being called to other duties. He knew he'd gone too far and that it would cost him dearly this time. He knew that the powers that be wouldn't go easy on him. But he didn't expect to be sent to what they called the "word pit"!

He went to explore his new place of work, the local newspaper office. The sight of these offices with their yellowed walls, rough tables and wobbly chairs, rooms that looked like a military barracks in a war zone, shocked him—he who had had the good fortune of working in United Media's sleek, new facilities. But it was mostly the reproachful gazes, the gazes of the young journalists who had nicknamed him "The Hare"—the only one who always got away with saying what he thought, whatever the circumstances. These young people's gazes seemed to be accusing him of treason, of abandonment; their eyes interrogated the reason for his presence among them, in the newspaper office's small jungle. Someone gave up his chair for him; he took it, thanked him with a nod, and put his briefcase on the table. Khasia immediately experienced a sudden attack of claustrophobia. He needed to get out, but he needed to do it without losing his dignity. The room was still silent. All eyes were turned toward him. He got up again, looked around the room, then picked up his briefcase and headed for the exit under the young reporters' silent applause. He raised his fist at the door without turning back.

Khasia knew he wouldn't last long with nothing to do; he could never sustain the inertia.

"Take me with you," he told his American friend Joe Clark, when he had had one beer too many. "You realize the offense I was fired for was lack of opacity? Can you tell me, you, mister press attaché for the American Embassy, you who have worked in every country in the world, can you tell me what lacking opacity means in journalism? My director told me that I was not original enough, that I understood nothing about my country's development policies."

"It's about African specificity, man. Where's your sense of humor? You're disappointing me, Khas. We are the people of the word, the fathers of the word that is in the beginning. We subvert words. We create them. We crush them when they annoy us. Where I come from, it's young people from the ghetto who, with their word, get America dancing while enriching Madison Avenue. They're the ones who make our language pulse by forcing it to bend to their daily lives, to their own rhythm. What can I say, man, an offense for lack of opacity is an offense for lack of opacity," said Joe, doubling up with laughter.

Khasia stared at him blankly.

"You know," Joe continued, looking more serious, "it was Emily Dickinson who said in one of her poems, 'Tell all the truth but tell it slant — /, ... the Truth must dazzle gradually / Or every man be blind.'

You never understood that, man. You never understood how to survive. You weren't able to see the omnipotence of the gods. That's why you were fired. That's our collective tragedy."

"I know that," murmured Khasia. "That's exactly what old Bila was saying. She would have made a very good journalist in our country, your Emily," he sighed, draining his glass. "And you, Joe, in your country, in America, do people obscure the truth, do they bend it a little so it suits the perspective of those who hold the reins of power?"

Joe looked at him for a long time without saying anything, then quietly, as if to himself, he said, "All those who have chosen the path of truth, all those who speak the truth 'with rectitude,' as my mother often says, eventually end up paying a heavy price. Many have paid with their lives. In your country too, Khas, here in your place, many have paid with their lives so that you and I can be here. Are you prepared to pay, Khas? Are you prepared to pay the necessary price? If you can't play in the big leagues, friend, don't linger there."

Though he was slightly drunk, Khasia stiffened, as he used to do in the old days before the teacher's stick landed on his unruly little buttocks. But he didn't stiffen enough; Joe's words hurt him like a slap in the face. He understood what Joe meant, but he never understood it as clearly as he did now that he had been fired.

"You know what I call people like you?" Joe sniggered. "I call them 'soft balls.'"

Khasia almost fell backward. He got up, lurched toward Joe, his hands in the air as if he were invoking the heavens.

"Now you must be the one who's drunk, my friend. You're delirious. Ever since I got out of school, I haven't stopped denouncing the abuses in this country with any of the means at my disposal. Me, I don't need any lessons in courage. I do have balls!"

"Then why are you asking me to take you with me?" Joe shot back. "You're not the only person who had an eccentric old professor. Ours used to say, 'With truth, you can go anywhere, even to prison.'"

"You know the word 'survival'? It exists in your vocabulary, this word, huh?" Khasia replied, blood rushing to his face. "There are no social services here, in case you haven't got that yet. Here we don't collect unemployment, we beg. Observe your surroundings, why don't you, Mr. Diplomat."

"So, you're leaving like all the others," Joe replied placidly, "You're leaving to enrich a world already sated, you're deserting the battlefield."

"For us these days, leaving is surviving. It may also be helping those who stayed here to survive," Khasia responded wearily.

"So there's the hero bringing the petrodollars back to the fold! And you think you're impressing me with this stuff, poor boy?" Joe added. "There's your problem, your eyes are glued to your belly like everyone else here. You need to eat, sure you need to eat! You need to take care of yourself, but everyone's so caught up in this belly dance that no one makes the time to organize the threshing and planting for the next seasons. That's what I've come to understand, since I've been here," he said, looking disgusted. Then in a hushed tone, he continued as if to himself, "And who's burying your dead? Who's clearing all these fields left perpetually fallow? There'll only be ruins left, my friend, when you come back, if ever you come back. Lianas will have invaded everything, tied up and paralyzed everyone. The ruin that began when my ancestors were torn from this land does not have to go on."

A heavy silence settled between them. Since he'd left television, Khasia was spending a lot of time with Joe. Together, they drowned their worries in martinis and Ella Fitzgerald. But their conversations had become stormier lately. Khasia had often left Joe's place, slamming the door shut behind him.

"Stop lecturing me, Joe," he told him during one of their evenings soaked in local beer. "What are you doing here yourself, huh? What are you fleeing, what are you looking for? The battle isn't won in your country either."

"Why do all the problems over in my country always have to be solved, before I have the nerve to stick my nose elsewhere? Is that it, Khas? The little black kid from the ghetto who's got the nerve to talk about international affairs, or even about his ancestors' continent? What sacrilege. That's it, isn't it? Just say it, that's what you mean," Joe fumed.

"You're pathetic when you launch into melodrama, Joe; it doesn't suit you. You know me and you know full well what I mean."

"To hell with you, Khas, to hell with you, you and all those who think like you. All of you with your self-important air, that idiotic, princely air."

"That's the beer going to your head, Joe. Don't accuse me of all of the troubles of your subconscious. I never talked to you in that manner, although others might have. It's an entertaining speech. It's the road we are to take together that counts, Joe, you know that, and those among us who have yet to understand this, over in your country and in mine, are caught up in this belly dance, as you say, the banal, futile dance of the immediate, the dance that someone staged for us several centuries ago."

One night when the two friends had spent their time listening to jazz and drinking corn beer while discussing what Joe called "global rot," he exclaimed, "God I'm so happy. I'm so happy, Khas, and I feel you're happy too, even if you refuse to let this happiness take possession of what my people call your soul."

He stopped for a moment, then added, "Yeah, your soul, man."

Khasia almost choked. He couldn't speak.

Before he could utter a word, Joe continued, "I know what you're thinking, I know you think I'm another black American who's dreaming, or even, as you often say, that the drum has intoxicated me. But there are things you'll never understand about people like me. Africa is a strange place, man. Africa is like me. At once glorious and pathetic, like all spectacular things."

"You're right, Joe, but this time it's the corn beer that's gone to your head."

"I'm very serious, Khas, I'm really serious. When I'm alone, face-to-face with myself, I catch myself thinking and creating very beautiful, very original things. When I'm alone, face-to-face with myself, confronted with the mirror of my own eyes, I love myself. I really love myself. But I don't like the reflection of myself that I see in other people's eyes. I don't like what people do with my ideas, my creations, and I assure you there are days that I don't love myself. Since earliest childhood, I've always seen myself through others' descriptions. You know, it's like the mirrors with two sliding panels that you find in bathrooms. Sometimes the one on the left is slid over the one on the right, and sometime it's the one on the right that's slid over the left one, and sometimes it happens that both are side by side. And I still don't know what is the best way to look at myself."

Khasia had closed his eyes and was swaying his head lightly to Sarah Vaughn.

"Do you understand what I mean?"

"Yes, Joe, I understand what you mean, I can even feel it a little. I understand we're all clowns. What's that word again? Schizophrenic?"

"No!" Joe shouted, slamming his fist on the table. "No, Khas, you didn't understand a thing, you'll never be able to understand, and you're not even trying!"

He sat back down and added more calmly, "There's less need to move the mirror around over here, it can remain longer on the left side, the side of the heart. Despite the problems, despite the crises, a reality that's thousands of years old remains here to nourish you. Do you understand that, Khas?" said Joe in a barely audible voice.

"I told you I understood what you said, Joe. I swear to you I understood. I may not experience it as you do, but I understand that the juxtaposition of angles is less frequent here, and that this may be more restful for the mind. But look at us: who are we aping? Who is being valued in our country these days? Certainly not the village elder. The mirror may not slide over often, but the situation is worse because it's stuck in the wrong place. In your country, Joe, you may no longer have the envelope, the shape, but you've retained the essence. You yourself often tell me, 'Go to the meat, man.' You've retained the substance. We here who think we're living in the maternal bosom, we no longer know where the milk comes from. Look carefully, Joe, and you'll see that we no longer know how to dig. We are on our way to becoming puppets."

Then, after a long silence, he sighed, "It's good to have an envelope, a shell. It protects, its veils, it defines, it even sets the tone, but God only knows it can also prevent any movement, any creativity, any action. It even stifles you sometimes. It's no surprise the tortoise takes part in so few games, no surprise it's so heavy-footed."

Joe had fallen asleep in his armchair.

That morning, Good Hope Center was buzzing with activity. Assumta was at the cash register, where she reigned as usual, teasing one person, cajoling another. Her gaze always turned toward the door and she welcomed every newcomer with a kind word. The fine observer she'd become always picked up on important aspects of the customer's physical appearance or even his personality.

"What will you have, beautiful?" she called out to the young woman who had just stepped into the bar.

Bella turned around to see if there was someone behind her to whom the lady at the counter was speaking.

"It's you I'm talking to, beautiful, what will you have?"

Suddenly, Bella began to tear up. She felt slightly dizzy and would have fainted had Assumta not rushed over to support her. Since onlookers were starting to come in, Assumta led Bella behind the bar, toward her bedroom. She noticed while supporting her that the young woman had no arms. Once Bella was seated and had regained her spirits a little, Assumta asked her if she was hungry. Bella shook her head no, trying to hold back the tears she was unable to control.

"You may be pregnant, you know?" Assumta teased, smiling.

"That's impossible," Bella whispered weakly. She began crying even more, and rising, asked Assumta to untie the knot fastening her *boubou*. Assumta complied, and Bella wiggled her shoulders so that the top would fall off. It slid down to her hips, revealing arms cut just above the elbow.

"You called me beautiful," she said in a slightly firmer voice. "How can you call me beautiful? Can't you see I have no arms?"

Assumta looked at her intently.

"When you stepped into the bar, I saw a beautiful face, a beautiful figure, skin like moonlight, and, above all, eyes bathed in peanut oil. How can you think you're not beautiful with such a gaze, which all women fear in a rival?" Assumta shot back, smiling. She continued, "What's your name?"

"Bella."

"You see, I was right. You are as beautiful as your name!"

In return, Bella's smile illuminated her face.

"You are ravishing, Bella, with or without hands. You have the face of a princess," Assumta said, drying Bella's cheeks. "Tell me, where are you going?"

"I don't know," Bella whispered. "I really don't know. Tingui, maybe."

Assumta looked at her for a long while. She could already see Bella caught in the shackles of Tingui's streets. Her face made it clear she knew no one there. Assumta also knew that, like hundreds of other girls before her, Bella was dreaming of finding, in Tingui, that miraculous cure for broken soul.

"You can stay here a few days if you like. We have room."

Bella dissolved into tears. No one had talked to her in this manner since her accident. No one, except her mother, had shown her as much solicitude. She cried for a long time, like she did when she was very small, her face buried in Assumta's bosom.

Khasia hadn't been back to Good Hope Center since his last altercation with Assumta, who, in fact, blamed herself for alluding to his past as a journalist. "Yet he seems so sure of himself! I should have known this wound was much deeper than he let on," she thought. She missed her daily talks with Khasia. He was the one who kept her informed of the latest national and international news. Khasia took pleasure in summing up the news for her—two-month-old news from the periodicals that took forever to reach him. He was happy to have such an engaged listener.

Assumta had taken the first step, sending a plate of *pèpèsoup* over to Khasia's house every evening. He was humbled by this gesture, and recognized Assumta's great maturity and tact. "Every time there's been a conflict, she's chosen the path of negotiation; she's always known how to bring problems back to their proper dimensions," he thought. He sent the plate back, washed, with the price of the meal, despite the protestations of the child who brought him his dinner. Assumta's instructions were clear: under no circumstance should the child accept payment from Khasia.

"If only she knew I'm not mad at her. If only she knew she'd forced me to face my life," he often thought to himself.

But the reason he came back to the bar was, first and foremost, more curiosity than anything else. He wanted to see the beautiful woman about whom everyone was talking. He wanted to see the most beautiful eyes and most enchanting smile in the world. As his friend Salla had told him, "She doesn't have any arms, but that's not important at all. If she says yes, I'll marry her tomorrow."

This had piqued Khasia's curiosity.

"You? Marry someone? None of the women in this village have succeeded in having you make up your mind, and now you want to marry a stranger? You who like your *foufou*, your *gombo*, and make fun of me when I cook, you're going to marry a woman without arms?"

"Why not? You have to see what she does with her feet. I'm going to learn how to cook. For her I'm ready to do anything. On second thought, I'll find someone who'll cook for us. You must see her, Khasia. No, in fact, better not. You'll show up, and with your look, she'll forget all about me."

"She'll forget about you? So you talked to her already?"

"No, not yet, but I sense she knows my feelings."

Khasia burst out laughing. His young friend fell in love every other day.

Khasia's curiosity got the better of him, and so that very evening he found himself returning to the Center. The corner of the counter where he usually sat was already taken, so he sat in a recess at the far end of the room, and waited for one of the girls to bring him his *pèpèsoup* and usual tonic water. He sat with his back to the wall and was able to observe Bella at will, while appearing to be looking out the window. Bella was in the midst of a great discussion with a driver. When she finished her conversation, she turned around and scanned the room, and without hesitation, made straight for Khasia, who, between mouthfuls, had his nose buried in his newspaper.

"Good evening, you must be Khasia. I am Bella."

"Is my name written on my forehead?" Khasia joked.

"No, but I was told you were the only one who read while he ate. Nobody's done that since I arrived here." Khasia smiled. She'd said this spontaneously, naturally. He liked her direct style.

"It's a bad habit I acquired long ago and can't seem to shake," he continued.

"It's not a reproach, you know," she replied, half-laughing, half-teasing.

"Alright then, good evening, Bella, or should I say, Moon. I've been told some people call you that."

"Proof we are all well-informed in Khala-Kanti," quipped Bella.

Khasia appreciated her sense of humor.

"Assumta is traveling. She asked me to have some *pèpèsoup* sent over to your place tonight, but since you're here, it's taken care of."

She said she hoped he'd enjoy his meal, smiled at him, and made her way back behind the counter, swaying as she walked.

"It's true this woman is striking," Khasia said to himself. "Her smile would make the stars dance. And on top of all that, a good sense of humor."

Khasia's visits to the Center resumed as before. He now took all his evening meals there, and given Assumta's increasingly frequent absences, Bella became his preferred listener.

She didn't make light of either his concerns or his theories about local and national development.

"You see, Bella, no one attaches any importance to local potential. Khala-Kanti is certainly getting increasingly renowned because of its *pèpèsoup*, but also because of its girls. Who is aware we have the best basket weavers in the country? Who knows the legend of the pierced basket? What are we bequeathing our children here?"

Bella could have listened to him for hours. She felt as if she had a walking encyclopedia within her reach. With sadness, she thought back to the time when she walked off with all the prizes for French in middle school, she thought about all the dreams that had evaporated when she became pregnant. She asked Khasia a lot of questions about every topic, history, politics, and geography. Everything interested her. The main highways were of particular interest, especially since Khasia had explained to her how the new Khala-Kanti was born. In her he found an insatiable listener. He passed on to her all the old weekly publications his friend Joe had been sending to him from the capital. Together, they analyzed recent world events. The freshness of Bella's point of view, her perspicacity, never ceased to amaze him. From time to time, Assumta threatened to forbid Khasia from coming, saying, "You're not at a radio station here. Don't chase the customers away."

Bella started reading avidly, or perhaps ardently would be a better word. Whenever she had a minute, she immersed herself in reading an article she deciphered with the slow pace and application of a child memorizing a lesson. She became indignant about conflicts that were a year old. She relished victories that had become obsolete because the negotiations had ceased and the conflict had resumed.

Unaware of the jolts of global geopolitics, Bella lived current events at her own pace, or rather bent them to suit the rhythm of her daily life. She forced events to linger, as if to redress the wrongs caused by their ephemeral character, as if to help them survive in the media's vertiginous world. Isolation made the bloodiest conflicts take on the character of fairy tales devised to frighten adults.

Every time Assumta was away, Khasia stayed on late at night to help Bella close up shop. This little ritual emerged naturally. They talked about everything and nothing, and sometimes a comfortable silence settled between them. He watched Bella go about her late-evening chores with wonder. "But how does she manage it?" he thought to himself. He'd once made the mistake of trying to help her open the refrigerator to put the beer bottles away. She'd shot him a determined look and proudly straightened up with a brusque movement that clearly indicated that she didn't want his pity. He opened his mouth to protest, but understood right away that it would be useless. The look in Bella's eyes and most of all, her gestures, were more eloquent than her words, as if her lack of arms electrified each of her movements with increased intensity. He would have so much liked to broach the subject of her accident, but she rarely gave him the opportunity to do so. In the middle of a conversation that he cleverly tried to steer toward her past, Bella continued to talk as if she didn't get the hint.

Since the afternoon when she had collapsed in Assumta's arms upon arriving in Khala-Kanti, she had not told her story again. Assumta had just explained to Khasia that Bella wasn't born disabled, but rather that she'd been the victim of a serious accident. Assumta had ignored the inquisitive look in Khasia's eyes and he'd understood that he better not insist.

Bella's grace, her smile, and the beauty of her face made one forget that she had no arms. She used her feet with the dexterity of an experienced yoga practitioner. Under the bar was a series of stools on which she sat to perform various tasks. She opened the fridge by sitting on one of them, and working the handle with her right foot. She got a bottle from inside, placed it on the floor, and then with her toes grabbed the bottle opener, securing the bottle with her left foot to open it. All this took place at great speed. The customers were all full of admiration; no one ever made any inappropriate comment; that was unthinkable. As soon as you entered the bar, the Venus-like quality of this woman hypnotized. With Bella, you could only be surprised, seduced, or respectful.

After hours, on the rare occasions when she sat down, her gaze darkened and Khasia invariably asked her what was wrong.

"Oh, nothing," she replied. "I may be a bit tired. It may also be this singer's voice. It's so sad. What happened to her?"

"You want me to stop the music?" asked Khasia.

"No, I like her very much. There's something at once comforting and sad in her voice. One of these days you'll have to explain to me what it is she's saying."

And so a ritual settled between them from the day Khasia noticed that, as soon as the last customer had left, Bella rushed over to lower the sound on the record-player, a gesture that was immediately followed by her rotating her head and shrugging her shoulders several times as if to release the tension accumulated throughout the day. To see her at the bar and to see her sometimes even dance a few steps, one might have thought she enjoyed herself in this noisy atmosphere.

"I thought you liked *soukouss*," Khasia said one evening.

"In small doses, yes. But not like this, at top volume, and day in, day out."

"So why don't you stop the record-player from time to time?"

"And the ambience, what do you do about that? Customers are looking for liveliness. They're in a quiet place all day. At night, they want to move."

"So for the end of the evening, I'll bring you music that's more soothing," said Khasia. "I'll have you discover women I like very much."

That was how the ritual with Billie, Ella, Sarah, and their sisters was born. After everyone left, Bella in the big wicker chair with her chin on her knees and her eyes lost in the distance, plunged into this unknown music in which she found familiar echoes. Bella melted in the music. She dove into it voluptuously. Sometimes she smiled at Khasia, but from time to time, he would catch a glimmer of sadness in her eyes.

"What is she saying?" Bella suddenly asked Khasia.

"She's telling us about her Blues," he replied.

"What are the Blues?"

"Let's say she's telling us about her sorrow, her sadness. She's telling us about her broken love."

A shadow passed over Bella's eyes.

"What happened to her? She seems to be crying. The sound of her voice tells me she's shattered in the deepest reaches of her soul."

"Yes. They loved each other very much, she and her man; she's saying their love could have contained all the loves in the world. He told her that her eyes bore the softness of dusk, and her body was the body of a Nubian princess. She called him her king, her sunny prince. Then one rainy night he left, and since then she's been waiting for him, sitting by her window, scrutinizing the face of every passerby. She's waiting for her prince to return as she listens to Miles Davis and 'Someday My Prince Will Come,' all day long."

"Her voice is rising, it's becoming harder, she seems angry at someone."

"Yes, at the evil tongues who say he's been seen in town, wearing a zoot suit, with a voluptuous starlet on his arm."

"And here, her voice has become soft again."

"Yes, she's repeating that their love is unique, eternal, that she is indeed the Nubian princess and he is her sun prince, and that she will wait for him her whole life, with her cat and her vodka."

"What a tragic fate. Did this really happen to her?"

"Who knows? Maybe yes, or maybe it's a text she composed to express the feeling of abandonment that arises from losing a dream."

"She fell, her wrapper came undone, and the calabash she was carrying on her head broke," Bella whispered.

The full moon set the little village ablaze with complicit intensity. It was one of those iridescent evenings that invited one to chat, and instead of closing up the bar that night, Khasia and Bella sat on the front steps. Bella, knees drawn up under her chin, leaned against the post that supported the railing; eyes closed, she breathed the music still playing in the bar. Khasia thought she'd fallen asleep, and as he was about to announce that he was leaving, she asked him, eyes still closed, "And who's singing now?"

"It's Billie Holiday. She has a poignant voice; she too is very sad. Everyone knows her story. There's a tragic fate for you, a broken fate."

Bella understood fate's ironies, its tricks and mockeries. Her beautiful face was glowing; she looked even calmer than usual. For his part, Khasia was overcome by a desire his febrile body had trouble concealing, but he held back lest he frightened her.

"O what beauty!"

"Who?" asked Khasia. "Billie Holiday?"

"No," Bella replied. "I meant the moon. It's stunning. It's music made image. I can almost hear it."

"Me too," said Khasia. "It is woman's kiss to the earth. Look at its lips curled in a big circle."

Bella burst out laughing.

"What's so funny?" Khasia asked.

Bella declared, "They are not her lips, they are her genitals. The moon is the perennial sex. The moon is a woman. That's why all the men in the world try to penetrate her, to get her pregnant. That's also why she bleeds every month."

Khasia smiled. "Bella will never cease to surprise me," he thought. Then he also closed his eyes, carried away by the blessed abandon that the fairy-tale atmosphere of this lunar night brought him, and most of all, mesmerized by this mysterious woman. Never had he felt so good in his body or in his mind. Never had he felt this enchanting well-being that made him feel as if he were floating.

Khasia whispered very low, almost as if speaking to himself, "A man is walking alone in the street. This man loves, he has lost his mind. The crowd, in its fury, was throwing stones at him and he, he spread flowers on whoever would have them. He was telling anyone who would listen that he was madly in love with a woman, a woman with a forehead as wide as the world, a woman with eyes as big and deep as memory, a woman with lips as wet with sensuality as freshly turned earth."

"This story's not as sad. Is it another song by Billie Holiday?"

"No," Khasia replied. "This time around these words are those of the Peul prince."

"The Peul prince! Who's that? And who is he talking about?"

Without batting an eye, Khasia answered, "He was talking about you."

"He was talking about me?" said Bella, bursting with laughter. "Who is this man? You did say Peul? I've never met him."

"He knows you, my Venus. He has always known you, and if you open your eyes wide, if you look up there in the sky, you will see him, beautiful, tall, and strong in his *gandoura*."

Bella straightened up, worried. She was waiting for Khasia to smile, to laugh, to reassure her, to tell her that he was pulling her leg. Khasia inched back on the step.

"I can assure you that he, the Peul poet Ousmane Diagana, is here. Listen carefully. Late at night, when the earth goes quiet, listen to the wind, listen to the evening breeze and the insects rustling: you'll hear him."

"Then he should talk to me himself," she said.

"But he did! He lent me his words, and made me his spokesman."

Bella began to smile. And joining in the game, she added, "You'll thank the Peul prince for me and also tell him that if he really knew me, he would have seen my amputated body and understood that I will never mark a lover's face with the seal of my hands."

"But he knows, Diagana knows, since he's talking about it," said Khasia. "Listen to the poet's voice, listen to the bard's voice.

"I would have liked to take your friendly hand and keep it inside mine, softly and fervently, for a long time.

"Spurred by some obscure desire, I would have liked to examine its lifeline and admire its finesse and beauty that are enhanced by the fire of the prayer bracelet and the enigma of henna-scented signs."

Then after a long pause, as Bella wasn't reacting, Khasia added, "But never mind that. I will read on your forehead as wide as the world all the secrets of your body and my hands will become yours under the knowing gaze of the queen with a thousand hands."

"But where on earth did you go to get all these words?" Bella gasped, heavy tears running down her cheeks.

Khasia knelt before her. He tenderly cupped her face in his hands, and with the back of his hand, lightly brushed away her tears. How could he make her understand that he felt her suffering, that he wanted to make it his so as to lighten her pain! And, especially, that he saw the promise of hope in her eyes. He whispered to her, "My Venus, you are my Venus."

Then resting his forehead lightly against hers, he murmured, "Tonight by your side, tenderness has bruised my body, deafened my senses. Tonight by your side, love has dissolved into tears to water the earth after the long night of drought. Tonight by your side, I lost my mind in the contemplation of your adorable face, which holds the world's seven wonders."

Bella had stopped crying. Her head was resting on Khasia's shoulder. Their hearts were pounding in unison, beyond all the lost and found illusions of their lives. Khasia's body urged him to take her in his arms and bring her home, but he was afraid, afraid that she might disappear once again behind the high wall she'd built for herself. He was concerned his male body would betray him too much. He wished he could have gotten rid of it for a brief instant, the time needed to assure her that they were bound by fate, and that the nimbus of her soul gave her mutilated body an incandescent beauty, that by her side he was rediscovering life's inspiration. He pulled his forehead away from Bella's with a gaze he drew from the inmost depths of his childhood. He embraced her with a thousand invitations for dreams, desires, and hopes. Bella understood this silent message. She could no longer recognize her body, a mutilated body that she had believed beyond repair, a body she'd thought dead. A sudden panic seized her. She didn't know how to react to the thrills of pleasure she was feeling. She no longer knew how to read her body's signs, nor how to hear the echoes of other people's bodies. She meant to get up, but at the same time the warmth of Khasia's head, now resting on her lap, held her prisoner. And so, in order to escape the thousand contradictory thoughts that jostled in her head, as they had once in the hospital, she closed her eyes and immersed herself in a profound, protective silence and fell asleep.

Assumta was intrigued by Bella. Every day she told herself that it had to be the ancestors who had sent her, especially since her own health had begun to decline. In her, Assumta found the friend, the sister who she'd never had. She had confided in Bella the details of her life in Tingui, details she had never dared confide to anyone else. She spoke to her at length about the man who had taken her to Tingui, promising her the moon, but whose pathological jealousy and violence made her flee. She even confessed that the allure of easy money might have led her to hang around in Tingui for much longer than she should have. When she left the man who took her to Tingui, her neighbor Tékla gave her shelter. But she left almost immediately because the neighbor's husband was coming on to her. Then she made new friends, old street hands who introduced her to harbor-side prostitution. "Sailors pay well," they told her.

"That's how I started going under the street lamps around the harbor and the big hotels in Tingui," Assumta told Bella one evening as they were sitting in Assumta's bedroom. "At the beginning, it was exhilarating. I had lots of money. I bought anything I wanted. I sent money back to the village. Then, with the onset of AIDS, the expatriates who were the best payers ventured less and less into the streets. You had to be connected to keep on working in good neighborhoods, and since I knew none of the go-betweens, I went down to the poorer neighborhoods. Over there, when clients didn't want to pay, they just beat us. While fighting with one of them, I got this long scar over my left breast. It may have been the ancestors punishing me for sullying their names."

"No!" Bella said fervently, "The ancestors don't punish in this manner. All you did was make do."

Assumta looked very tired, her face tense with the pain of the disease that was gnawing at her. She was tortured by the memory of the indignities she'd experienced. For the first time in a long while, Bella wished that she had arms so she could wrap them around her friend. She watched her intensely. In that look, she put all the power that eyes can convey. She looked at her with compassion, with love, with gentleness. And she repeated, "I assure you, the ancestors do not punish—they cannot punish in this manner. And what about me? What have I done to deserve what happened to me? It's the madness of mankind," she added in a low voice, as if to better convince herself.

"Thank God my friend Tékla was there to help me. She couldn't tell her husband she was coming to the hospital to take care of me, otherwise he would have beaten her. She brought me food every time she could. She was the one person to tell me over and over again that even lepers' parents don't throw their children out, in order to convince me to return to the village," Assumta mused. "For a long time I didn't dare come back here, to Khala-Kanti," she continued. "I was ashamed. But the injuries to my body were so grave that I decided to come home. I didn't want people to find my body by the side of the road. Most of all, I didn't want my family to reject my corpse. This happened to two friends of mine who contracted AIDS. That was the moment I panicked. It's no fun finding yourself with a friend's body at the outskirts of a village from which you're being chased."

Assumta kept quiet for a long while, then went on, "It's ironic, you know. I don't know how I managed not to catch this cursed disease in Tingui during all those years. I come back to the village, move in with one man only, think I'm safe, and then I catch it. It was here, hidden in the shadows, this wretched disease, watching me, waiting for me so that. . ."

Assumta did not finish her sentence. She continued her explanation. "My father never asked me anything. He gave me a plot of land and let me be, but because of my injuries, I had a lot of trouble working in the fields.

That's when the big strong guy came to the village."

"And what about Clarisse and the others?"

"It's a long story. These women each carry their own baskets of the problems of this world. What's important is that they're well. We're all well. Even Marie, who came to die here, is well, too. She is free from her pain and from the gaze of others. Ask them, talk to the girls, they'll tell you," Assumta said.

Then she added, "We are as women of the same lineage. We've become a kind of sorority. As for the others, the three girls who hang around with the drivers, you know their stories as well as I do. But you know what, darling girl? Tell yourself there's no such thing as chance. Don't be fooled by chance: it doesn't exist."

Assumta looked very tired. Bella didn't dare ask for more details about her illness.

Despite her jovial air and her conviviality, Assumta was, deep down, very secret and solitary. Other than Khasia and Bella, few people in the village really knew her, even though she talked to everyone, had a kind word for each person, and as a good shopkeeper, had a smile and a flattering word for every customer. Yet, she was wasting away in plain sight, spending entire days in bed, convulsing with coughing fits and plagued by various other ills about which she said little.

Each time she began to weaken and to fail, she left for the capital. Laughing, she liked to tell Bella that she was leaving for a fattening-up treatment. But Bella eventually understood that the reason she was leaving so frequently was to keep people from gossiping, to keep people from deserting the Center, which had become her life, her second skin. She was prepared to do anything to preserve the only place that brought her a modicum of dignity.

"I'm leaving for Tingui again tomorrow. Can you take care of the Center?"

"Yes, as usual, you can count on me, Assumta. Do you know when you'll be back?"

Assumta hesitated a long time, opened her mouth as if she were about to say something, and changed her mind. She said only, "I don't know, it'll depend.... You know, this nasty disease is capricious, pernicious. Either it bruises you and drains you completely, as in my case, or else it gives you a reprieve and tricks everyone who comes in contact with you. And no one knows which spirit guides its moods."

Bella didn't know what to answer. Near tears, she ran toward the door. But Assumta called her back and invited her to sit near her. She plunged her hand in her bosom and pulled out a handkerchief rolled into a ball, which she carefully unfolded. A small key was nestled in its folds. She took it, and opened the lock to the old trunk, in which sat two iron boxes.

"Here is my life," she told Bella. "This is where I keep all my money and all my important papers."

Bella was very ill at ease. She didn't quite know what to say. She was deeply moved by the great trust Assumta was showing her. It brought tears to her eyes. Every time Assumta traveled, it was Bella who managed the cash register. It was Bella who placed the orders and made sure the restaurant was closed at night. She put all her heart, all her energy into it. She was even more demanding than Assumta herself. Everything had to be perfect. Assumta had to be proud of her little world. When she came back, Bella gave her a detailed account of what had taken place in her absence. She knew what the Center meant to Assumta, and in her own way, through small, ordinary acts, through the ardor she brought to her work, Bella tried to thank her. A hundred times a day she looked for ways in which she could thank the guardian angel that fate had placed in her path. A hundred times a day she tried to make the whole world forget she had no arms.

"As you can see," Assumta said, "these papers are in an old trunk. If someone came here to steal, he'd make straight for the nice Vuitton suitcases. People know I'm a coquette. No one would think of coming to nose around in this old trunk."

Bella smiled, she was getting to understand Assumta's methods pretty well.

"You remember what they used to tell us in school, don't you? There's always someone smarter somewhere else."

She closed the trunk, knotted one corner of the handkerchief, in which she slid the key, then folded the small handkerchief fourfold and asked Bella to come close. She caressed her face, held her tightly against her and said, "From my bosom to yours." She plunged her hand in Bella's dress, wedged the handkerchief in her bra, under her left breast. Her hand lingered there for an instant. She closed her eyes and moved her lips, and removed her hand. Then, settling in her bed, she turned her head so Bella wouldn't see her tears.

"Let me remember," she thought. "Let me experience again and immerse myself in these nights when the hopes we had buried deep inside our souls were reborn. Let me experience again these evenings when the earth confirmed to us that we are her offspring." She heard the singular, melodious sounds of those dream nights. Once again she saw her mother bent over the sick women who haunted their house like emaciated shadows. She saw again her administering the steam bath that healed from the most powerful spells. And once again she saw her mixing bark, sap, leaves, branches, all she could draw from the body of a tree to extract salutary potions. "Mother," she said, "hold out your hand to me. Hold your protective hand out to me. Hold the blessed and beneficial hand you inherited from the ancestors out to me. Beseech on my behalf all the healing masters from the hereafter. Ward away from my body the shadow that is besieging it now. Bathe me in heavenly waters. Come closer to me. Kindle the dying flames of my body's fires. Mother, mother!" she implored.

Her body became lighter, lighter, and became lighter still. And, with the spirit of her mother, she felt herself leaving her body. Together they kept watch over her young body that reflected an incandescent light akin to that of rosaries that glow in the dark. The room was bathed in darkness. The only illumined spot was the bed where the young woman with the glowing body was lying. Then all of a sudden, they heard the clinking of the cowries tied around the dancers' ankles and the steady beat of calabashes.

Assumta sat in the center of a large, luminous circle. There she was, her face tense with pain, her gaze intense, her eyes feverish. Across from her was her mother, healing staff in hand, surrounded by her sisters in battle. Together they uttered incantations, they pleaded with the ancestors, they implored their pity. "My daughter was called prematurely!" Assumta's mother yelled. "They had the wrong door." She was brandishing her staff toward the heavens. Her body entered into a violent trance. The opponents' arrows were unstoppable, but as an experienced healer, her body knew how to fend off the blows she received. She gave a few of them as well. The duel lasted for hours. Despite the leaping, the tumbling on the ground, despite the shouts and rattles, despite all of these desperate mother's secret gestures, the bird of death, a funereal owl with overdeveloped eyes and ears that never gave its prey a chance, clung to her shoulder. The healer suddenly turned into a lioness. She roared. She growled. She thundered. She showed her claws to ward off the other lion that was attacking her, a soul-eating lion. But the bird of death was still there, perched on her shoulder, staring at her with his big, placid, indifferent eyes. And the healer collapsed, her hands tied. Her assistants, her sisters, the clan of women with whom she'd surrounded herself for the ultimate ceremony, carried her away and disappeared into the early morning mist. She didn't even dare look her daughter in the eye.

Assumta's body entered into a sudden trance. Another coughing fit came over her, shaking her entire body. She let out a rattle and arched her back, her bosom was on fire, a thousand spears and thousands of needles pierced her loins, someone was holding her waist in a pincer and her neck was caught in a vice. Her body had become a war zone under assault from visible and invisible soldiers. Then, little by little, her body calmed down, her breathing became steadier. She curled up and fell asleep.

Bella was still there. She'd watched the convulsions as they took possession of her friend's body. She'd seen Assumta's body bend with pain and hadn't been able to do anything. She hadn't even been able to offer her the most banal gesture. But she'd stayed up for hours, a silent witness to the duel between her friend and death. With her eyes, with her breath, with her fighting stance, an erect, upright posture, she'd given her friend all the comfort she could. She'd sealed a life pact with her that even death could not obliterate. Having made sure that Assumta was in deep sleep, she lay down next to her friend, pressed her body against hers, and in turn fell asleep.

Seated on Véro's veranda, the three cousins were teasing each other. It had been a long time since they had gathered together. Despite the stifling heat in Tingui that day, Assumta was wrapped up in one of Clarisse's big winter sweaters.

"It was God who had you come back to this country. I would never have found such a warm sweater here. Thank you," said Assumta, smiling at her younger cousin.

"I would have preferred for your God to help me to stay over there. I didn't want to come home under these circumstances," Clarisse replied. Smiling, she added, "But I am happy to be with you."

They evoked their childhood. They remembered the petty larcenies they had committed while on vacation at their grandparents' in Khala-Kanti. Once again they saw their mothers' annoyed faces. With long silences and revealing sighs, they wondered about the turns their lives had taken. Clarisse, the adventurer, had found herself in France without papers. She had hung around here and there, taking menial jobs, then had gotten involved in prostitution, like several of her girlfriends.

"It's not the paradise people had painted for me," she told them. "I thought I was going to get rich very quickly and even find a husband and come back to this country to open up a shop. Still, I saved, I sent money over so they would keep it for me and...."

She did not complete her sentence. She was shaken by sobs. Véro came near and gathered her into her arms.

"Come now!" she said. "You're not going to cry every time you tell this story, are you? You've been here for two months, and you still cry every day. If you go on like this, you won't have any tears left to cry over me," she said, teasing Clarisse.

Véro was the eldest of the cousins. Since the death of their mothers, Véro had become the elder of the younger generation, at whose house everyone gathered when things went poorly. It was at her house that Assumta stayed during her long trips to Tingui. Véro had lost her husband a short time after they were posted to Tingui, but the offices of the Imprimerie Protestante, for which he used to work, had let her continue to use his company-provided residence. Her sons' school was around the corner, and she worked nights as an accountant for the printer. She had thus been able to maintain a decent standard of living. Assumta helped her by sending her provisions from Khala-Kanti and helping with the children's back-to-school preparations. Véro accompanied Assumta to all her doctor's visits. Together they crisscrossed the capital's markets in search of the rare packs of Retrovir and Viramune that the smugglers were offering at better prices than the pharmacies. For an entire year, they'd tried to thwart this disease. They'd experienced moments of hope when Assumta regained strength, when color returned to her face, and she went back to Khala-Kanti again. But this last return was different. Although she hadn't said anything, Véro knew that Assumta had understood there would be no other pilgrimage to Tingui. Exhausted by the new treatment she was under, she could barely leave her bed. The small household lived at the pace of Assumta's rare words and great suffering.

"I can't take it anymore," she told her two cousins one evening. "Take me back to the village."

"Wait another month," Véro replied, "and if you're not feeling any better, we'll talk about it again."

It had been almost three months since the two women had this conversation, and Assumta's health had not improved. Late one night, as Clarisse was helping her put on her night robe, Assumta held her hand and whispered in a barely audible voice, "There's room for you at my Center in

Khala-Kanti. Come live with me."

Clarisse didn't want to upset her.

"Of course, Assumta, I'll come take care of you. I have nothing to do here anyway."

"No, that's not what I mean. Being there will do you good. It's not the village you knew in the old days. Things have changed a little, you know, and intelligent as you are, you'll be sure to find a way to get by there."

"Oh no! I'm done with men," Clarisse replied, misunderstanding Assumta.

"No, no! That's not what I mean. It would take too long to explain. Just come and you'll see. There's a woman there with whom I think you'll get along very well. She's the one managing Good Hope Center when I'm not there. And anyway, if you don't like it there, you can always come back here to Tingui. But don't stay here," she implored, "you'll get eaten alive. Ask Véro to tell you my story."

Clarisse didn't answer. She didn't want to contradict her cousin. She could see that pain was contorting her face. You could feel she'd made a tremendous effort to speak for that long.

"Have Véro come," she whispered.

Assumta's eyes implored, as Véro came into the room. Véro understood her cousin's request immediately.

"Now?" she asked, coming close to the bed.

Assumta nodded yes.

It was almost midnight when Véro's car came to a stop in front of Assumta's restaurant. Clarisse wanted to get out immediately, but Véro held her back by the arm.

"Shhh," she said, "she's sleeping."

Indeed, Assumta had fallen asleep in the back seat. Everything around them seemed calm; the silence broken only by night's ordinary noises. So the three women let themselves be gently rocked for more than two hours. But when a coughing fit shook Assumta again, the two cousins hurriedly got out of the car to help her to her feet. Each woman held her on one side, and enveloped by the night, they made their way forward like forest shadows. They pressed themselves against each other instinctively. Assumta's gait was more assured than expected. The three of them succumbed to a fit of hysterical laughter as they recalled the sacred nights of their childhood. Once they'd calmed down, they noticed a small light in front of the bar.

"I can see something moving," said Clarisse.

"Come on, stop frightening people," Véro replied.

"No, I swear, look!" Clarisse insisted. "You see, it looks like there's someone on the steps."

Three of them froze. Indeed, you could see something moving in the distance, a shape that seemed to move toward them.

"They're back—the masked beings!" Clarisse cried.

"You were always the one standing in front during these ceremonies," Véro whispered, her voice trembling. "Go ahead. Go on forward. Go see what it is."

Clarisse held on to Assumta, who was now walking with a sure step, as if Khala-Kanti's nightly perfume, whose secret this small village kept, had invigorated her. In turn, the shadow froze. Assumta was still moving forward. Then she recognized Bella, who pounced on her. Both of them flopped onto the ground. Assumta was staring at Bella's face. She wanted to ask her what she was doing awake at this hour, and Bella wanted to reply that for a while now, she had been waking up with a start every night, her heart in her throat, and she had kept a light on in front of the bar's door, waiting she knew not why, moved by some irrepressible force. But no word was uttered. Instead they exchanged a long, eloquent look, knowing they were bound by a tacit understanding, a complicity between them born of first encounter. Khasia was waiting by the door.

"You've begun my wake, Bella," said Assumta. "That's it. They must have told you in your dreams that my hour has come!"

"What? What are you saying?" said Clarisse.

Assumta shook her head no. Then, turning to Khasia, she said, smiling, "I see you've become Bella's shadow; I told you this woman sticks to your skin!"

Khasia burst out laughing and held Assumta tightly against him.

"You recognize them?" she asked him, pointing to Clarisse and Véro with her chin.

The darkness of the night kept Khasia from clearly making out the faces. He signaled that he didn't.

"You remember my young cousin Clarisse, the bold one? There she is, in fact, and next to her is her big sister Véro. You may not remember her; she didn't come to Khala-Kanti as often as Clarisse did."

Khasia kissed both women. Everyone was happy to see Assumta talking cheerfully. It was a good sign. As she was beginning to cough again, Khasia carried her and took her to her room. He laid her on the bed with great care, as one would put down a newborn baby. She didn't weigh much more than one of his little schoolchildren. Khasia was moved to tears. He looked at Assumta for a long time, looking at this body curled up in a corner of the big bed, a nearly inert body, and thought back to the pretty young woman who was Khala-Kanti's life and soul. And his heart sank. He kissed her hair, as he'd done that evening long ago when they'd fought, then came out of the bedroom and disappeared into the night. The three women wedged pillows on either side of Assumta's frail body and took turns waiting, until the waiting was no more.

Bella mourned Assumta like she'd mourned her arms. She told Khasia that, this time around, it was her heart that had been amputated.

For her, any pain was directly linked to her body, and she often asked Khasia to blow on her heart as if to soothe the burn caused by Assumta's passing. With cold-water compresses and fans, Khasia turned himself into a healer of broken souls, succeeding where more than one cardiologist would have failed. In doing so, he held Bella back from the precipice of desolation, reminding her of her own role as a light bearer. For Assumta's sake, Bella determined to live and threw herself into work at the Center with boundless zeal and devotion. But since Assumta's death, another face had increasingly insinuated itself into her daily life. The fateful day she had almost succeeded in erasing from her memory was haunting her again; and from time to time, when someone entered any room she was in without making a noise, she gave a start and let out a cry of panic.

A long, strident cry tore through the usually calm atmosphere of the small neighborhood in Maéba. Aboutou threw the axe she was about to strike against the wood and cried out instinctively. Her mother, who was doing laundry behind the house, rushed over at once.

"What? What's wrong with you? You hurt yourself?" "No, Mema," said Aboutou, her heart beating.

"But I heard you cry out twice," the old woman continued, gasping.

"But I only cried out once, the first cry came from over there," Aboutou said, pointing to Boualo's house. "It sounded like a cry of death, Mema."

"That's just what I was about to say myself," the old woman continued. "I even thought for an instant that you'd dropped the baby."

"Mema, how can you say something like that?"

"But what can it be?" the old woman went on. "Most people are still fishing or in the fields at this time of day. Unless it's Bella's little one! She's had this nasty fever, for more than a week now, the one that took away your other godchild last month!"

"I'm going over there, Mema," said Aboutou at the thought of her friend's daughter being desperately ill. "I'll be right back."

"Oh no, you're staying!" Mema replied. "If the baby wakes up, you'll be able to feed him. I'm going."

So the old woman took the path that led to Boualo's and Bella's home.

"Bella, Bella? Where are you? Answer me," Mema shouted as soon as she saw Bella's small wood-frame house.

But no one answered. There was no perceptible movement. Everything was silent. When, out of breath, barely able to stand, she got to the house, she nearly fell over backward seeing Boualo coming out of the kitchen, his pipe in his mouth. He was busy cleaning his machete.

"But, Boualo, you didn't hear me calling?" she asked, looking anxious.

Boualo didn't answer, which worried the old woman even more. He had an evil look in his eyes, the same look he displayed after his legendary fights with Bella. An unhealthy calm emanated from his person, Mema thought.

"Where's Bella? And the little one? We heard someone cry out, we thought she wasn't well," Mema said, breathing heavily.

Boualo remained indifferent, carrying on with his cleaning. When he was done, he threw the rag he was using to the ground, went back into the kitchen, then came back out with his climbing belt and an empty palm wine gourd, and headed toward the road without a glance toward the old woman. She hurled a few insults at his back and called him a disrespectful son. It was at that moment that she heard faint moans coming from the side of the house. She headed in that direction, telling herself that little Mialo had crawled to the bathroom by herself and might have fallen into the septic hole. But the spectacle before her eyes took her breath away. She howled, rasping and guttural, from deep within her chest. Then the images became jumbled and she collapsed to the ground.

Hearing the cry, and recognizing her mother's voice, Aboutou also cried out. "That's it. The little one is dead. She's dead. The little one is dead!" Poor Bella, her only child, she thought. Securing her baby on her back, she fastened her wrapper around him and in turn rushed toward Bella's house, calling, "Mema, Mema! Bella, Bella! Where are you?" She rushed toward the house, but saw no one. She headed toward the kitchen, no one there either, but as she came back out, she noticed the rag soiled with blood. Her heart started pounding. She decided to go around the house, and what she saw released from her a cry as hoarse as her mother's. She staggered, held on to the wall. "My God, my God, my God. Don't let me fall down. Don't let me fall down on my child!" She put all her strength into this invocation, took a deep breath, and began crying out again for someone to come to the rescue. "Come, oh! Come, oh! They're dead! Who's here? Come, oh! Someone please come!" she sobbed.

She sat in the middle of the pool of blood in which the two women were lying. She picked one of Bella's arms up and held it tightly against her heart. The other arm was lying at the young woman's feet. "My God, my God," she sobbed incessantly. She heard steps drawing closer. Stunned horror was written on every face. Some fled, horrified, some fainted on the spot, others stood frozen in place.

"Someone go get her mother; she's in her field in Natika, I saw her pass by this morning with little Mialo," a neighbor said.

"What happened? Who did this? Where's Boualo?"

Questions were flying from everywhere. Two men helped Aboutou to her feet. Her wrapper was covered in blood.

"I don't know! We heard a cry, Mema came to see what was happening, and I followed her shortly after, and here's what I found."

Someone tried to move Mema; she let out a barely perceptible moan.

"She's not dead. She's not dead. She moved!" one onlooker shouted.

"Bring some fresh water," said Bosco.

He splashed water on the old woman's face. She came to, surprised to be surrounded by all these people.

"Stay back!" Bosco said. "Let her breathe."

Little by little her memory came back, and she explained that Boualo was cleaning his machete when she arrived.

"He didn't even speak to me, he stank of death! He's the one who killed her, I saw his eyes!"

"Someone go to the police station. Essia, go to my house get my motorbike and rush to the police," Bosco ordered.

Like many young people in Maéba, Bosco had also returned to the village after the layoffs at the Chocoprat factory in Tingui. Back to square one, he used to say, holding court during his regular late-night sessions with the two or three clients who no longer had enough energy to launch into a frenzied *soukouss* or enough money to buy the drinks that bring a smile to an interested young woman's lips.

Life in Little Maéba revolved around Bosco's bar and the fish market located by the seawall nearby. Big Maéba, some twelve miles away, had over the years become the country's Little Riviera, the place where many expatriates fled at week's end. A few charming, small hotels were scattered along the coast, and many of Little Maéba's inhabitants, who had turned themselves into guides, took tourists on the hunt for the exotic, out to the small inland villages. And for the few Westerners who wanted some local color, a stop at Bosco's had become a mandatory ritual. They came back out unsteady on their feet, their stomachs and minds bloated with beer and *soukouss*.

Bosco was one of the rare young people in Little Maéba to have made a successful transition back to the village. He'd tried setting up something with Boualo upon the latter's first return to Maéba just before the soccer World Cup, but still in thrall to the lush future he was already living in his head, Boualo had shown little interest. However, since his second time back, Boualo was in the bar every night, always seated in the same corner, speaking little, his nose in his beer. Bosco had brought him home blindly drunk more than once.

The sinister ballet of Boualo's return home unfolded in stony silence.

Bosco knocked on the door and half-asleep, Bella let him in. Together, they undressed Boualo and laid him down on the bed. Bosco then shot Bella a questioning look, which she answered with a shy smile and a barely perceptible shrug of her shoulders. Bosco closed the door softly and left without uttering a word. Seated on her bed, head between her hands, Bella cried until she too fell asleep. Bosco had touched her hand only once. He'd held it very tightly in his as if to convey to her the urgency of his desire, as if to tell her that she could find something better elsewhere.

Bella hesitated for a moment, then softly withdrew her hand from Bosco's hold, eyes brimming with tears. Bosco looked at the woman to whom he'd promised the moon and stars, he looked at this beautiful woman who all the young people in Maéba used to fight over. He looked at her standing in a puddle of illusions, in front of that even bigger mirage that was the man lying on the bed behind her, in this house with faded walls, and he too felt like crying. "What a waste," he sighed to himself before withdrawing.

He left out of respect for her, because he knew she was right, because he knew she was trying to preserve what little dignity she still had. Only once had Bella asked him for money. "It's a loan, I'll give you your ten thousand francs back," she promised. And despite his protestations, she had paid her debt little by little, over one long year. He had loved her all the more for it.

As usual, Bosco reacted instantly, while several people, still in shock, appeared to be seized by a sort of paralyzing inertia. Dazed, they were circling Bella's body. "If her father were still alive, Boualo's head would have fallen already," they said. The crowd parted to make way for Dama, Bella's mother. A neighbor tore Mialo from her arms and moved away from the scene. Dama collapsed onto her daughter, lifted her torso, then immediately raised her head and cried out, "But she's not dead! She's not dead! Her heart's still beating, someone bring me some water, we need a car, do something, Bosco, do something, we need to take her to the hospital!"

"I already asked Essia to go get my motorbike," said Bosco.

As if she had not heard Bosco's response, Dama continued her internal dialogue.

Then she declared with maternal certitude, "Yes, yes, I know, she's still alive." Bosco didn't dare tell her that he'd sent the motorbike to fetch the police, instead of taking Bella to the hospital.

Dama kept on splashing water on Bella's face. She had had someone bring sheets, in which she wrapped her daughter. The motionless Bella now lay on a mattress set directly on the ground. A few yards away were her two arms, immersed in the basin of fresh water she had drawn that very morning. Obeying an irrepressible instinct, Dama started rocking her daughter. She sang to her the lullabies of childhood while the crowd stared at them with indecent curiosity, captive witness to a private ritual.

Drawn by the noise of an approaching vehicle, everyone rushed to see what was coming. But recognizing the sound of his motorbike's engine, Bosco announced this was Essia on his way back from the police station in Big Maéba.

"Let's hope their car is following him," he added.

Indeed, Essia was accompanied by a man everyone immediately mistook for a medic.

"What's happening here?" he asked, parting the crowd.

The sight of Bella's bloody body brought him to a standstill.

"Oh my God!" he cried out, looking terrified.

Bella's mother, whose dress was covered in blood, asked him if the police van was coming.

"The van wasn't at the station, but I asked that my colleagues follow me here as soon as they're back."

Dama threw herself at the policeman who, taken by surprise, rocked backwards.

"Then why did you come?" she shrieked, "Why did you come? You don't know where the van is? I know where it is, your damn van. It's in the bush buying game and plantains for your wives while my daughter is dying! And you didn't think to commandeer a car? Weren't you told someone was dying?"

She was pummeling him as she spoke. Two sturdy fellows had a hard time prying her away from the policeman.

"Calm down!" implored Bosco. "Calm down!"

"I'm going to report this lunatic; she'll see what happens when you assault an officer of the state!"

Hearing these words, Dama once again rushed toward him. All the hatred she felt for the people who controlled her existence as a market woman in the capital returned to her in force. She thought back to the never-ending negotiations between the policemen and the bush taxi drivers, the only ones who were willing to venture out into the small villages. She thought back to the "dues," the infamous pay-offs the drivers had to make to the policemen daily for real or invented violations. Pay-offs that, in turn, they included in what they charged their passengers. As a result, obviously, the price of a trip fluctuated with the sum that had been handed over to these bribe-eaters. Dama thought back to the hours she spent silently moping in overheated cars, barely seated on one buttock. Hours during which she held back her tongue, knowing that just one inappropriate remark from a passenger would mean that the trip would come to an end.

"You want to report me? I'll give you a reason to report me, you bribe-eater! Do you know he stinks of alcohol, this bum? He was probably in a bar, drinking!"

Someone held her back firmly this time, while Bosco asked the policeman not to make the situation worse.

"Take her to the hospital, Bosco, she's going to die. Put her on your motorcycle, please!" Dama begged.

"But how? She needs to be able to hold on to me, otherwise we'll never make it!"

"Put her on your back, put her on your back like a basket. You know, just like we carry our babies!"

And so this was how Bosco got to the hospital, sweaty and bloody, with a dying Bella on his back.

The nun who admitted them to the Catholic mission's small hospital located at the very heart of Maéba crossed herself at the sight of Bella's dismembered body. Bosco quickly explained the situation to her as two nurses placed her on a stretcher. "The arms are still in the village. We're waiting for a car to bring them over; we put them in a basin of fresh water," Bosco concluded.

"They won't be much use," the nun said simply.

The news of Bella's arrival got around the hospital quickly. Even the other patients lined up to see the woman whose arms had been cut off by her husband. A thousand versions of the story were circulating. Before he left the hospital, Bosco even got an account of the dismemberment scene by someone who swore she was present at the time of the incident. "It's her co-wife who cut off her arms," the woman claimed.

Even the hospital security guard had found a way to make a little money. For a hundred francs, he let in curiosity seekers.

The only official person who came to talk to Dama about what had happened to her family was the journalist from the new weekly *Le Noyau*. He had come from Tingui specifically so he could speak to her. This reassured Dama. They must have sent him so that justice could finally be done, she told herself.

Dama told her story to this man, who seemed full of compassion. She spared no detail, thinking this would do justice to the memory of her daughter, who had been in a coma for a month now. To the woman in the next bed who asked her whether she feared reprisals for criticizing the police and the Ministry of Justice's inaction and discrimination, Dama replied, "My daughter was pilloried. She is the sacrificial lamb. Justice did not uphold us, because we have nothing, because we are women. I fear nothing. When you remove the intestines from an animal's carcass, there's nothing left. So what should I fear?"

The surprise in Bella's family was immense when her picture appeared in the paper's humor column with the title, "Women Beware!" and the sole caption, "Man cuts wife's arms after she refuses to tie goat outside." Aboutou, who came to see Dama at regular intervals, did not have the courage to tell her in what context Bella's story had been published.

"But when is this story going to be printed?" Dama asked incessantly. "People need to know what this criminal did. People need to know that no one came to our aid. That Maéba's policemen spend their time swindling people—people need to know! I told this journalist everything, I saw him write. He wrote a lot!"

She paused for an instant, then continued, tears in her eyes. "And to think he's still walking around, this bastard Boualo. He's still hanging around Maéba's streets. He would never have dared do that when my husband was alive. His head would have been chopped off already, I can assure you."

Aboutou comforted her as well as she could, trying to take her place by Bella's bedside from time to time. Aboutou also reassured her as to her granddaughter's well-being. She had been taking care of Mialo since the incident.

"Don't worry about Mialo. She's my goddaughter, after all. What's more, she's adorable. It's a joy for us to have her in our home. I swear, Mema Dama, don't worry about her."

"I've buried too many people, Aboutou. First Bella's little brother, then her father—I cannot bury my own daughter. I don't have the strength for it. I won't make it!"

And yet, Dama held on through all the months of her daughter's coma. She quickly adapted to the routine of a patient's aide. Like all the others, she first brought her oil stove, her bag of rice, and her tins of tomatoes and mackerel, and on the days when no family member came to bring them something to eat, she did some basic cooking in the hospital's backyard. Dama quickly made friends in this small community of ad hoc nurses. A few benevolent neighbors showed her the ropes. After these brief respites from Bella's bedside, her powerlessness seemed even more palpable, more crushing to her.

When she wasn't tending to the small tasks that governed their daily lives, Dama sat by her daughter's bedside. Her gaze fixed on her daughter's face, she prayed silently, invoked her dead parents and implored all the gods she knew. Each time she returned to Bella's bedside, she was overcome by a heaviness. Her heart tightened in her chest and her throat constricted.

In these moments, it was always the same image that kept coming back to her. She saw a face. She saw the face that had been watching her, for as long as she could remember. She looked herself in the eyes and discovered with horror that she, Dama, was a carrier of death. Fate was pointing its finger at her. She had not conveyed the message of immortality to her daughter in time. In fact, she herself was a chameleon from time immemorial, a stutterer, who, for lack of healing words, had been unable to tell her daughter that death would not touch her, that she was a daughter of the waters, a daughter of all the seas in the world, and that she carried life within her. On the other hand, the bird, the bearer of bad news, that chatterbox, that tattletale of the forest, had a looser tongue and had brought the message of death, whereas life, a prisoner, was hanging at the tip of the chameleon's tongue.

Dama was sweating. She got up abruptly and moved, as if to escape these images, which were rising up from the deepest reaches of her childhood, from the innermost depths of her being. No, this was not the way death came to mankind. She, Dama, was not responsible for the grief of all of the mothers of the world. She was not the chameleon. She could not carry life and death within herself. Then she stood and walked the length of the room with assurance, as if to move away from the shadows of those people who were pointing their fingers at her, people who were whispering to her the fatal version of her story. She sat down again, took a deep breath, and resumed her narrative.

"The day you were born," she said, "the ocean opened and *Mami Wata*, the great mermaid of the waters, sent out her messengers to fetch us, you and me. There we found our grandparents, your uncles, your aunts, my best friend Nestine, all the faces I hadn't seen in a long time were there. *Mami Wata* presented us with a magnificent feast. She fed you coconut milk and cocoa sap. She pampered you all day long, you were so beautiful. Then she tried to keep you. She wanted to make you one of her little mermaids. But I rebelled. I told her that she didn't have the right to do this. I told her that it was time we went back home, even if deep down, I would have loved to stay there—we were so comfortable there. *Mami Wata* got mad. She made the waters rumble and the algae and fish tremble. Everyone cowered in front of her, but I held on. So she decided to punish me, to cut the bridge between the two worlds. She separated us from all the dear people with whom I had just been reunited.

"It was a great bereavement, everyone was crying, it took an army of mermaids to tear me away from my mother and Nestine. I was shattered. I was in profound danger. I didn't know what to do, what to choose. But when I looked into your eyes, when I looked at your luminescent eyes that contained all the promises in the world, I understood there was no possible choice. So she sent us away from her kingdom, but before that, she opened your heart and placed two pearls in it. One pearl was very beautiful, a nearly black shade of gray, the pearl of life, of happiness; and the other was dull, drab, and white, the pearl of misfortune."

Dama kept quiet for a moment, to give silence its turn. And when silence, in its turn, became quiet, she leaned over her daughter, caressed her neck, and spoke, "Loosen the rope around your neck, my child. Loosen it. No one is pulling it anymore. It's at your feet." Then, drawing intricate patterns with her fingers on what remained of Bella's arms, she whispered in her ears, "You are the chameleon. You're stuttering but you're not mute. The mythical word, the regenerative word is at the tip of your tongue. Get them out, these words. Don't be afraid. Get them out. Look for the sources of the breath in the arid and wounded areas of your body." Dama then settled in her seat like a pregnant woman who's nearly due, her being, her belly filled with maternal will and certitude, and waited nine months until the moment when her daughter most gently awakened.

Dama spoke with her eyes closed, indifferent to the crowd of patients and onlookers that had formed around Bella's bed. Without question or protest, Dama accepted the role of great priestess in a ceremony of atonement. Day after day, night after night, she nourished her daughter with communal breaths that carried the tutelary rhymes that had beaten the cadence of her childhood. And little by little, just as the doctors were beginning to lose hope, Bella began to move and even speak. Slowly color returned to her face and, from time to time, the permanent veil that covered her eyes lifted, and she could then be heard laughing. No one dared broach the tragedy with her. And never did she ask about or allude to what had happened to her. She didn't even ask for Mialo, her daughter. It was as if, like her arms, her past life had been severed from what remained of her after a year in the hospital.

In Tingui, right in the heart of the city, children were taunting a man and yelling, "Hey, Walk-Backward, how are you doing?" one of the kids asked the man, who was rummaging through the Hotel Mermoz's garbage. The man did not react. He continued his methodical search, putting his finds in an old blue bag that never left his side. When he had finished, he climbed out of the trash bin and walked backward past the children. The children followed in his step, walking backward as well. They all knew Walk-Backward. Other than the occasional battle he fought with some invisible enemy, he was rather harmless.

Boualo was wandering, his hands up in the air at times, at times around his neck, then in front of himself as if to ward off some invisible person. From time to time he held his arms as a screen above his head as if he were protecting himself from some kind of aerial attack. He was roaming from neighborhood to neighborhood, stammering the same words to his arms and hands. "Careful, don't touch me! I'm telling you, don't touch me!" he shouted while vigorously thrashing about. A crowd formed around him. He seemed to wish to strangle himself, his two hands tight around his neck. He was struggling as if these were hands other than his own, his forehead covered in sweat, his eyes bulging, his nose snotty. "Let me go!" he yelled, "Let my neck go! Tell her to let my neck go!" Then, without transition, he started laughing, laughing a full-throated laugh, squirming about in every direction, rolling in the dust, still shaken by a fit of laughter. "Stop tickling me," he gasped between coughing fits. "Come on, stop!" Then just as suddenly, he curled up and started sobbing loudly.

His old uncle, Manguila, sometimes came to get him on the occasions when he was notified that Boualo had fled from the mental institution where he was confined, the Maison des Rameaux.

"Come on, get up, Boualo, get up. They're gone. I've just chased them away."

"You see I'm right. You see I'm right. They're following me everywhere. They won't let go of me. They're keeping me from doing what I want. Chase them away, Papa Manguila. Chase them away," he begged, collapsing again.

"Don't worry, Boualo, I'm going to ask Bella to come get her arms. I saw her the other day. She promised she'd come."

These last words had the desired effect. Boualo got back on his feet, dusted off his clothes, and followed his old uncle, walking backward. Sometimes the uncle held his elbow to help him avoid an obstacle. Sometimes also, Boualo would turn around himself to assess the course, then resume his walking backward.

"She's gone, Manguila, she's gone. She's afraid. I'm watching her closely now, she won't be able to attack me from behind ever again," Boualo said.

Ever since his murderous act, everyone in Maéba had stopped speaking to him. Weeds had overtaken his yard; he neglected his farm. Sometime later, he turned up in Tingui at old Manguila's house, his mother's eldest brother, who seemed to be the only person to be concerned about his fate. Manguila put him up for months and later, when his crises began, took him to the Maison des Rameaux, the only institution in the country that treated the mentally ill. But there needed to be someone to take care of Boualo, someone who would live with him in one of the little rooms that served as residences for the patients. But no one wanted to see Boualo. The women in the family to whom such duties often fell wished him dead, having never understood why the Maéba police had released him after only one month in custody. "There were no witnesses," the police had claimed, adding, "No one saw him commit this act, and then his wife never came to lodge a complaint." Boualo retreated into a tenacious silence, opening his mouth only to repeat the same sentence over and over again:

"She wants my death, this woman. I don't know what she wants from me!"

And so Boualo escaped regularly from Maison des Rameaux and arrived at his old uncle's house stinking of urine and grime.

"Come on, quickly, Boualo, we're here. Go behind the house, I'll bring you some water. You need to wash."

"Take this wretched man back to where you found him!" shouted Manguila's wife as soon as he came into the kitchen. "Take him back, him and his evil spirit. I don't want any misfortune in my house."

Manguila did not answer. He came into the room, took a bucket of water and headed behind the kitchen, toward the sheet-metal structure they used as a bathroom. Boualo had undressed and settled on the big rock where the family sat to take steam baths. Manguila grabbed a hand broom of reeds, soaked it, and soaped it up, and began scouring his nephew. This operation lasted nearly an hour under Cicilia's disapproving gaze. Several buckets were required. The last step was the steam bath, a bath that seemed to calm Boualo down for a while. Manguila set a pot of boiling water in front of him. He'd had some citronella, leaves from guava and papaya trees, *massep*, and several other leaves to form a curative tincture that marinated a thousand healing virtues. These were the very same leaves Manguila's mother used in the old days to treat every disease from malaria to evil spirits. He covered Boualo with an old blanket and leaned him against one of the posts of the wobbly bathroom structure.

Manguila looked down at the lumpy mass of boy and blankets at his feet, and thought about his late sister. It was a good thing she wasn't here to see this. She would have finished her son off with her own hands. Exhausted, he closed his eyes.

"Pa Manguila, the voices are gone. I can't hear the voices anymore. They're gone," said Boualo, his body sweating.

The same scenario repeated at regular intervals. After a short stay with his uncle, Boualo gave the impression that he had recovered his sanity and would only talk about his childhood. His first bridge crossing with his grandfather, a man who'd passed away too early, but whose exploits Boualo's father had recounted to him. He also liked to remember his first soccer matches. As he perched victorious on one of his cousins' shoulders, he'd wave at the crowd that had come to cheer him.

In these moments, Boualo seemed normal. Then, when Manguila thought him cured, Boualo would suddenly begin to talk to Bella's arms again. Then he would disappear, leaving the old man perplexed. Manguila didn't understand the vagaries of life. How did his nephew's future, once so full of promise, come up so short? How could a boy whose success was almost guaranteed come to commit such a vile act? Where had the little Boualo gone? The little boy whose exploits in sports had given them the illusion that they, too, would be entitled to a few crumbs of affluence? Like Boualo, Manguila also remembered Boualo's famous regional championship victory.

The entire village was abuzz! Little Boualo, barely eighteen years old, had just scored the goal that would lead Maéba's only team to the regional championship. Since the arrival of the young prodigy, the child with blessed feet, Maéba Flèche hadn't lost a game. Newspapers were beginning to write about Boualo. For his part, Boualo's father could already see him playing for the national team in the World Cup, and even for a European club.

Vikoti loudly proclaimed this to anyone who would listen. He bought drinks for everyone, already celebrating the victories to come. He felt rich in advance, and spent his salary accordingly, to the great despair of his Boualo's mother. There was a rumor that the coach for the national soccer team would attend the regional game, scouting for young talent to round out his player list for the African Cup selection matches, whose winning team would then move on to the forthcoming World Cup.

In anticipation of the coach's visit, Vikoti didn't let his son out of his sight. He personally watched over what Boualo was eating. And it was absolutely necessary to avoid ill-intentioned spirits. Boualo's mother was stunned by Vikoti's attentiveness to their son. Boualo was her only child, the son for whom she'd waited for a decade. Vikoti ignored Boualo at birth because he already had two other children by his mistresses. Miraculously, this child had become the apple of his eye.

Boualo scored three goals during the regional championship final, giving the regional team its first victory of note. One week later, the coach came to see Boualo's parents in a car loaded with bags of rice, cases of tomatoes, beer, and champagne. He spoke at length with Boualo's father. Neither mother nor son, who joined them later, saw the envelope containing five hundred thousand francs that was discreetly slipped in Vikoti's pocket as incentive for Boualo to immediately join the national team in Tingui. Boualo's mother shyly asked what would become of his studies, and was told, "Of course we'll put him in a good school in Tingui. And if we qualify for the World Cup, we'll even be able to send him to France for accelerated training." Boualo was in heaven, but his mother didn't like this man's expansive manners. He spoke like a hyena hiding its teeth.

Despite his mother's reticence, Boualo's departure for the capital proceeded as planned. In the month before his departure for Tingui, Boualo enjoyed all of Maéba's attentions. He ate for free wherever he wanted and girls fought over the honor of keeping him company. Bella was shocked when the handsome boy built like a wrestler passed near her and looked her way. She was much too reserved to vie for the attention of the soon-to-be-champion. With this acclaim and hero-worship, Boualo left for Tingui to become a national hero.

Though he knew very little of the capital, Boualo had no trouble at all adapting to his new life. He bit into it wholeheartedly, as if following a course prescribed by an unavoidable destiny. As soon as they arrived in Tingui, the whole team was invited to stay in the Grand Hotel, fiefdom of all who counted for something in this world. It was in this privileged setting that the team would live while preparing for the African Cup play-offs. Every morning the players crossed town in a bus to get to their practice, surrounded by the screams and admiring looks of scores of young people who'd set up residence in front of the hotel. For their part, all the backers and people in high places were allowed to attend the night practices. And at the end of these sessions they handed out thick envelopes to the players who'd most distinguished themselves.

Bitterness and anger spread quickly among those who felt ignored by the visitors, and so in spite of the influence and power of these men, the coach asked them not to attend training sessions anymore. Boualo was the favorite of these gentlemen, and they did not refrain from singing his praises in front of his teammates. To entertain themselves after being banned from the practices, they took bets on the number of goals he would score during each of his upcoming games. He received compliments and was showered with gifts. In turn, Boualo achieved miracles on the field. He was the little prince with priceless feet, "Goldenfeet," as the crowd nicknamed him.

Boualo became, without contest, the new star of the national team. He was the favorite of the crowd, to whom he offered a feast of unparalleled athletic prowess at every match. His charming smile was not lost on the women attending the matches. In spite of this attention, his teammates couldn't accuse him of being arrogant or selfish. He willingly shared the small riches his admirers heaped on him. He was genial and teasing, but his behavior also displayed a certain smugness that exasperated his teammates. He claimed the team's successes as his own. Like his father, he was also already living in a post-World Cup period. He could already see himself in the European club of his choice and even envisioned frequent returns to his country as a national hero awaited by thousands of fans.

When the Sphinx National team won the African Cup, a match during which Boualo scored the two winning goals, he was even closer to living his dream completely. The Sphinx National had qualified for the World Cup, and the entire country was in a trance. Everyone was given a holiday to better enjoy this euphoria.

A nationwide crisis ensued when Boualo injured himself during a friendly match with a foreign team. He fractured his shoulder during a scuffle and had to be rushed to the hospital. The newspapers only wrote about him, the doctors' analyses, their prognoses—everything was broadcast in detail, and was often distorted and exaggerated. A specialist was brought over from France to care for the national shoulder upon which the entire country rested its dreams. People waited on Boualo hand and foot, and while he was frustrated by the shoulder that kept him from playing, he was happy to know that he was indispensable, fawned over.

As a result, he failed to understand the significance of the specialist's announcement. After three months of rehabilitation, Boualo felt ready to return to play, but the doctor informed him that his spine had been much more affected by the injury than they had originally believed. The specialist informed him that the least little fall would result in permanent paralysis. Boualo's world fell apart, and he sank into a deep depression.

In order to avoid hurting the team's morale a few days before its departure for the World Cup, the only announcement made was that Boualo was going back to his village to rest and he would join the others in Brazil later. This announcement triggered an avalanche of speculation. For some, he was finished, washed up, and they were getting rid of him by sending him back where he came from without the least compensation. "What about all the goals he scored?" his fans wondered.

According to the vast majority, Boualo had gone back to the village to recharge his batteries, to gird himself. He was the person who would receive, from the hands of Maéba's most renowned *marabout*, the protective ointments to be used by all players before each game. He was the one who'd been chosen to go to the village and give the ancestors something to eat. In its daily program about the World Cup, the *Tambour à paroles* devoted at least fifteen minutes per day to the Boualo story. Then the World Cup began and all eyes turned to Brazil.

Boualo's return to Maéba was glorious. People were in and out of his parents' home all day. He played the role of princely heir to perfection, lavishing attention on each visitor with the detached air that befit his status. But like all has-beens, he soon lost his freshness. His face soon reflected the worried look of the faces around him. His stories lost their juiciness— their joyful lightness—and became heavy with lassitude. The time between visitors increased, and the wine no longer flowed freely. Boualo's fortune and his appeal left him at the same time.

It was at this moment that he met Bella. She came, nearby, to visit a friend. Finding himself alone, Boualo had time to observe his neighbors coming and going. As a result, he noticed this pretty girl. He courted her assiduously. As his neighbor often said, "He chatted up the girl, dribbled her heart down-field, and scored."

Bella was very flattered by the attentions Boualo lavished on her. She was surprised to discover in him, contrary to talk about his prickly temperament, someone who was very considerate. For his part, Boualo was touched that this pretty girl would show interest in him at a time when most of the young women who had previously been at his feet had lost interest. Soon rumors went around that Bella was pregnant. People were already whispering that Boualo would soon discard her. Yet, to everyone's great surprise, Boualo came to visit Bella's parents to ask for her hand in marriage.

Sometime earlier, he'd found the courage to go up to Tingui to see his former supporters, especially those who'd previously showered him with gifts. Several of them had him cooling his heels in their waiting rooms. Others gave him a cold welcome. The World Cup was over, and even though the Sphinx had moved up to the one-eighth finals, Boualo's name had disappeared from people's lips. They were now talking about other new stars. Boualo came out of these meetings in a daze. He thought he was dreaming. Once again he could see all of the faces that adored him just a few months ago. He could still hear their promises. He could still feel the vibration of their accolades, yet, in less than a year, there was nothing left— no soccer, no work, nothing, not even the promised training.

At twenty-five, he saw life slipping out from under his feet. The meeting with his coach was distressing, and for the first time since his accident, he cried. He cried as he used to cry in secret, far from his young friends' eyes, after being spanked by his teachers. This time around, he cried while looking his coach in the eye. He cried while looking at the person whom he had revered, the one who held the keys to his future. He questioned him with his flowing tears. He reminded his coach that a promise was a debt. Unable to look Boualo in the eye, he moved about in his office, and using some urgent outing as an excuse, put his hand in his pocket, pulling out a few bank notes. "For your wedding," he said. "And as for work, I'll see what I can do. You can count on me."

Shortly after his wedding, Boualo returned to Tingui to take a desk job with Chocoprat, the country's sole cocoa factory. Bella, who had just miscarried, followed him some time later. They settled in the new middle-income housing that the factory built for its employees. Boualo benefited from the patronage of one of his coach's friends. Although this certainly wasn't the world he had dreamed of, it was better than the last months he'd spent in Maéba under his father's disgusted gaze, surrounded by the indifference of people who used to fight to see him. He argued with Bella less often and even got back in touch with a few former teammates who hadn't made a lot of money after the World Cup either. Together at night they'd visit Tingui's best bars to re-live their glorious past and imagine the future they'd been denied. They left the bars late at night, as pathetic and empty as when they'd entered.

After just two years on the job, large layoffs were announced at the factory. Since he was among the last ones hired, he was among the first fired. He was beginning to believe friends who'd told him that too much joy brought bad luck. Any period of calm, of respite, was a bad omen. Didn't his mother often tell him that some villages hadn't seen happiness for years? His neighborhood, his entire building, had just been struck by this misfortune.

Bella shook herself from the torpor into which her daughter's birth had plunged her, and began to look for work. She was prepared to do anything, but then Boualo began to take his frustrations out on her and let his pride get in the way of her efforts to find work. There was no way she could be a servant for one of the capital's well-to-do. Not his wife. Not the wife of the Sphinx National's best player. There was no way she could start a little business in the neighborhood either. It would lower his status almost as much. Their first big quarrel took place because Bella had the indelicacy to ask him what status he was talking about.

Eventually she started taking care of a few children in the building, whose parents worked all day. These parents were so satisfied that she soon had as many children as she could fit in their small apartment. Boualo hated this new occupation as well, but because Bella was working out of sight, he let her do it. He let her do it mostly because his search for work had been fruitless. Without Bella's work, they would have found themselves on the street.

Boualo began to stay away all day and came home late at night, his face closed, looking exhausted and distraught. Bella had learned not to ask questions anymore. One word out of her mouth would provoke a storm. Once, Boualo even accused her of not getting pregnant on purpose. "Doesn't everyone know that children bring wealth?" Little Mialo, born a few months before, didn't count. This child, with red hair, whose skin was a translucent white, didn't exist in Boualo's eyes. "This cursed child," as he often described her after a few beers with his friends. Ironically, she was a child who resembled him as no other daughter had resembled her father before. Bella called her Mialo, which in her language meant "As you wait for happiness." Bella loved her passionately. She breathed all the love her heart knew into her daughter's mysterious skin. She armed Mialo's unusual skin with love, tenacity, and courage. She sheathed her with the covering she would need to parry the blows life would hurl at her.

Little by little, Boualo withdrew into his own world. He sometimes brought food back home, as well as banknotes given by former admirers, but he still wasn't finding any work. The economic crisis was choking the country. Eventually, he started coming home later and later, sometimes resurfacing only at dawn, his breath stinking of alcohol. He collapsed on the sofa and fell into a deep sleep. With a neighbor's help, Bella would take him to their bedroom, and as well she could, restore some order in the main room before the children arrived. Sometimes she even went looking for him after he hadn't come home for a day or two. Once, the police brought him home, asking Bella to take better care of him. "You're lucky I'm bringing him back to you. We were about to lock him up, but the captain recognized him and asked us to take him back home. He assaulted the wife of a very well-placed person this morning."

"But why?" asked Bella, looking at Boualo.

"He was drunk," said the policeman.

"You shit! You son of a bitch!" yelled Boualo.

The policeman nearly pounced on him.

"What did you say? You called my mother a bitch? And you know who your father is, right?"

Boualo threw himself at the policeman. His colleague stepped between them, and with a severe look at Boualo, said, "We should have kept you inside today. That would have taught you a lesson."

"I wasn't drunk! I can hold my drink, I can. I'm not a baby! This woman splashed me, she dirtied my clothes, and so I, I reacted like a man. I threw a rock at her car."

Bella herself was also aware of these women and men who filled out their seats with their entire bodies, with smugness, and with contempt. Those people who looked at pedestrians as if they were guilty of being alive. Like all pedestrians in the capital, she clearly understood what Boualo was describing to her. Wasn't the dream of all former pedestrians to become drivers one day, so they too could fill the car out with their flesh? In the daily shoulder-to-shoulder struggle on the capital's jam-packed streets, people tried their best to occupy as much space as possible. Even in taxis the customers, who'd settled in before you, barely shifted one of their buttocks so you could squeeze in half of yours. The young captain, who himself had long been a pedestrian, understood Boualo's reaction perfectly. He refrained from smiling and had Boualo released after a few hours in custody.

Bella became concerned about the sudden influx of money into their household. Boualo bought new furniture. The refrigerator and the stove were brand new. He'd even bought Bella two beautiful dresses that came straight from one of the most expensive boutiques in the city.

"These two dresses are worth three times our rent," Bella noted while accepting the gift.

"Ungrateful woman! I can never do anything good enough for you," Boualo shouted before leaving the apartment, slamming the door shut.

One evening, however, unable to hold back any longer, Boualo confided to Bella that he'd just been admitted into an organization where veterans took care of new recruits.

"They take care of new recruits by giving them all this money? You sure it's not a trick where you have to sell one of your own?" asked a suspicious Bella.

"Don't tell me that you believe these things too! No, nobody's selling anybody," Boualo said.

"Then where is the money coming from? If this were some *susu*, you would have been asked for a contribution. They're either robbers or feymen," said Bella, frightened.

"I knew I should have kept quiet. I can never discuss anything with you. All they asked me was to introduce them to a few of my former team sponsors. They made me a canvasser and I'm the one who establishes contact. I introduce one party to the other and after that my partners take over," Boualo explained.

"And who have you introduced them to until now?" asked Bella.

"I'm to introduce them to the coach in a few days."

"And nothing has struck you as fishy in all this? You're being paid for work you haven't done yet and you don't find this strange? You're going to pay with your life! These people don't forgive!"

Bella's words seemed to have some effect on Boualo. He looked at her for an instant, appearing unsure, and then, collecting himself, he added, "What life? Because you think I have one? Without work? With this child of misery you brought into the world?"

Boualo knew exactly how to calm the feeling of uncertainty within. He knew that by hurling hurtful words at Bella, he could quiet the anxiety that gripped him. He hated his own lack of courage, the weakness that kept him from holding to account all those who had signed paperwork using his name, who had eaten and drunk using his name. He hated the paralyzing fear he felt in front of his father, his coach, all the men who had sold him at auction, had reduced him to poverty. With this new group, his blood brothers, as they called each other, he felt important again. These men he'd met through two former teammates talked to him like few had done recently. They treated him with consideration, with admiration, and above all, with the same respect people used to show him when he was Goldenfeet. "A big man isn't a small one," they often told him. "You deserve greatness. You've done so much for this country!" Boualo accepted their gifts even though they were said to have acquired their wealth in unscrupulous ways. He accepted their gifts with naiveté, with the same eagerness that had led him to accept the sponsors' presents, without even asking himself what the payback would be this time.

Still, he panicked when he learned that one of his Sphinx friends, a companion in his nocturnal rounds, the very man who had introduced him to this organization, had been locked up for extortion. Immediately, he decided to stop attending their nightly meetings. The response from his "blood brothers" was as immediate as their initial generosity. About ten muscular young men arrived at his house, grabbed all the furniture, the new stereo, the television, and any appliances they could find, and then they wrecked the rest, before leaving without a word. Boualo never set foot in the building again. At first, he didn't even dare contact Bella for fear she'd be forced to reveal his hideout. Bella survived in Tingui as best she could, but finally found herself compelled to join Boualo in Maéba, furious at herself for not taking the typing classes that would have certainly allowed her to find a position as a secretary.

"Boualo! Where's my bastard of a son! If you were a real Vikoti, you'd be part of a European club right now, and me with you," he said. "Your grandfather must be turning over in his grave seeing the wreck you've become."

Bella came out of the kitchen and rushed into the house. Her husband was sitting on one of the dining room chairs. She looked at him. As usual he was unperturbed by his father's invectives, his face drained of any emotion, devoid of any feeling, as if nothing could reach him anymore. Since his second return to the village, the shameful return, he'd found refuge in drink and silence. This reaction was exacerbated by the death of his mother. Bella headed toward the veranda to ask the old, visibly drunk Vikoti to go back to his home.

A small crowd was beginning to gather and Bella, whose temperament was rather discreet, could no longer stand being the neighborhood's daily show.

"You saw that? My son's lost his balls. He's sending his wife over to talk to me! Since my son doesn't know how to be a host, those who want to drink follow me home."

And he left staggering toward the bar, which wasn't far from his son's residence.

"Someone bring us something to drink. I must tell you what kind of man my father was."

His two "partners in brew," as his wife called them, were there as usual, spurring Vikoti on with words like, "Well said, my brother. Wet our gullets so we can better listen to you!" In this way, Vikoti's wife saw the money for her food ration and her two children's school expenses drain away.

"It was at the time of the construction of the bridge," Vikoti continued, intoxicated by the attention of his audience. "The bridge you cross to go to Big Maéba. My father was foreman. Yes indeed, he was responsible for all the workers. He was the first black foreman in this country!"

Someone let out an admiring whistle.

"Yes, my brother, man pass man! But ask me how he got this important position—him, the simple son of a farmer," said Vikoti.

"Don't make us salivate, Vikoti, just tell us."

"When the white men from the Zovatel Company arrived in Maéba, they asked the chief to find them some foremen. Of course, the chief wanted them to hire one of his sons, who must have been about twenty at the time. The white men told him his son was too young. The chief, who wouldn't have it any other way, then suggested his younger brother. But this one got fired after a month because he was often late. He'd just gotten married," Vikoti added mischievously.

Everyone burst out laughing.

"There's nothing like a new bosom to ruin a man's life," someone said.

"And so the white men decided to find a foreman among the workers," Vikoti continued. "And of course, my father suggested himself as a candidate. He was serious. He worked hard, and above all, he was a handsome man—tall, big, strong, and imposing. The white men chose him, which enraged a lot of other people who were eying this position. So my father arrived on time every morning, asked people to walk in a single line, and yelled the few French words he'd heard the white men shout to their employees. '*Aléan marse, abancez tousuite bandandouille!*' He made sure every one of them was at their job, and went about his usual rounds until the end of the day."

Vikoti looked at his audience to make sure everyone was listening closely. The effects of the alcohol seemed to have worn off. He was speaking with animation, waving his arms, stressing every one of his syllables. He had become his father.

"But of course, those who were jealous, especially the chief's cousins, who thought they were owed everything, couldn't stomach my father's success. You yourselves know there are always people who like to put their mouths in other people's business. A delegation went to see the white man to tell him my father was a bad foreman because he didn't know how to read or write French. 'Boss, he never takes roll call in morning. He holds the sheet of paper, but he can't read the employees' names.' They told this white man everything. I'm telling you, they told him everything. Of course they were suggesting the white man replace my father with one of the chief's young cousins who had just received their Certificat d'Etudes Primaires Supérieures. The white man said he would come to roll call tomorrow morning and that if he wasn't happy with Vikoti's performance, he would replace him with someone else."

"Can you believe those people? Betraying their own brother like that!" Vikoti's two companions exclaimed in unison, good listeners to a story they'd already heard many times.

"Listen, listen and you'll understand my father's genius. As you know, when there's too much water in a container, it overflows. That very night, someone let my father know what was in the works. And my father had everyone he knew very well among the workers, most of them his friends' sons or his young cousins, come to him. He asked them to place themselves among the first in line when the construction site opened the next day. Nobody saw anything wrong with this, especially since it was always in good taste to get along with the foreman. The next morning, my father was there, baton in hand."

Vikoti stopped to better savor the effect of his story on his audience.

"My father, who had never worn glasses, meticulously pulled a case from his pocket. With calculated slowness, he opened it, extracted from it a small pair of glasses that he placed on his nose, adjusted them, took the list of names and began his roll call, calling by name the workers he knew. 'Malam, Bokomb, Beyo, Pele, Manguila, Nobejo.' Then, when he didn't know a youth's name but knew his father's, he said, 'Son of Entembo, son of Tamal, grandson of old Amos.' And when he'd forgotten a name or when he didn't know the person, he yelled in our language, 'And you, there, what are you waiting for? You want me to come carry you?' 'And you, sleepy head, get moving!' Taken by surprise, everyone imitated the person in front of them, responding 'Present!' and walking toward his post while the white man thought that my father was continuing the roll call."

"A real man, your father," someone said.

"More cunning than the turtle and the hare combined," someone else added.

"Indeed. That's how my father kept his position. Later, the government even awarded him a medal of honor from the governor because he'd risked his life to save one of the white engineers who almost got carried away by a torrential flood. I was with him the day they awarded him his medal. I was the one who, in front of the entire village, read the governor's letter to my father. The white man in charge of the construction site told my father I'd go far. Yet when I finished school, first in the entire district, they sent one of the chief's sons instead of me. My father never got over that," Vikoti concluded, his eyes misty with tears.

After a long silence, he continued, "And you know, of course, who this chief's son is. Mister the Postal Service Minister. He's a cabinet minister today, a cabinet minister, instead of me! This good-for-nothing—why? Because his name is Elagal. Since when have Elagals been chiefs here? One of these chiefdoms devised by the colonizers, I'm telling you. If only he'd deserved to be sent to the William Ponty Teacher's College in my place," he sobbed.

Most of Vikoti's audience had fallen asleep, but the old man kept on talking. Holding his head between his hands, he was reliving his youth. He'd never left Maéba and had worked his whole life as a treasurer for the company that ran the harbor. His inordinate love of women had earned him a large progeny. An excellent public speaker, he always knew how to conquer women's reticence, and most important, he knew how to sing his own praises. He described his own status with so much conviction that many women looking for someone with money let themselves be taken in by his story. Over sixty, he had just married a young woman who could have been his granddaughter. She in turn had just had twins, and when the prison that was his own house became too narrow, when the small community of children he'd spawned and their mothers turned into annoying sergeants-at-arms, Vikoti sought refuge in Bosco's bar where, after a few bottles, he recovered his eloquence and his cantankerousness.

His young wife came to get him and took him back to the house.

"You love me. Tell me that you love me and that you're not going to abandon me too. I'll be a cabinet minister one day, you'll see, and when my Goldenfeet wins the World Cup, I'll buy you beautiful dresses," he whimpered incoherently.

Makrita supported him all the way to their bedroom and turned her face away to avoid his fetid breath. She undressed him, put him to bed and lay next to him, pressed the palms of her hands together and began to pray.

Assumta had not been mistaken. Clarisse immediately liked it in Khala-Kanti. She often said to anyone who would listen that she buried the wreckage of her life in this corner of the forest where greedy liana and trees snapped it all up in one night. No one suspected that this inveterate city girl, this Afro-Parisian, would so happily return to life in the small village. She eagerly clung to the hands that were held out to her, and plunged into life in this luxuriant domain with pleasure.

Clarisse was very sorry that Assumta was no longer present because, in a matter of months, Assumta had succeeded in helping her to restore her deep taste for life. By facing her illness with serenity, Assumta had given her a lesson in courage, but more importantly, Assumta rekindled in her a passionate desire to live for herself and by herself.

Often, at the end of the day, Clarisse sat, and sometimes knelt, in front of Assumta's grave. She would talk to her cousin, as though she was still by her side. She weeded around the tomb and cared for the flowers that she had planted. Sometimes she pulled a well-worn notebook out of the pocket of her *kaba*. Her face shone radiant as she read from the text, something that seemed to bolster her faith and hope in life and living. Then, as she surveyed the rich vegetation surrounding her before making her way back to the Center, the notebook would vanish into the depths of the pocket in her *kaba*. She loved these calm moments when there was communion between what she could hear in her heart and what she could see with her eyes. What she felt was all so real she could almost touch it. She would then walk slowly back to the Center, calm and peaceful as a lizard taking advantage of the last rays of the sun.

But one day Bella saw her charging back down the path.

"That is incredible!! To shit near a grave!! What an insult! Come see this, Bella."

"What? What has happened?" Bella asked.

"Come! Come and see this for yourself. They have soiled Assumta's grave. People don't respect anything in this country anymore."

"But there is a toilet right behind the bar."

"Yes, there is a toilet, but that does not prevent them from pissing just anywhere. But from that to going all the way to the tombstone to shit . . . I am fed up, Bella! Things must change!"

And that is how, thanks to Clarisse, the Good Hope Center became a rest stop unlike any other. There she set up monitored urinals and pay-toilets—something unheard of in the country. Everything there was neat and clean. These were simple pipe-toilets, where the persistent smell of the disinfectant cleaner Cresyl, better known as *bola to ndjé* ("do whatever you want"), emanated from a hole in the ground. Cresyl erased the traces of any disgracefully smelly visit.

A few yards from the toilets, Clarisse placed her wicker armchair in the shade of flame tree where, as a charming hostess, she patiently waited for her customers to exit. After each visit, she inspected the toilets. If she came back with her nose pinched, the customer got a sharp talking-to about the deplorable state of his digestive apparatus. "Your belly's dirty! Your visit will cost you a little more," she'd tell the guilty party. Then she splashed the entire space with *bola to ndjé* and thoroughly washed around the toilet. She then went back to the customer who was waiting for her and ceremoniously pulled her bottle of *Bien être* from the big black bag that never left her side, and made the culprit sniff a few drops of the eau de toilette.

"Come on, breathe in. It'll do you good. The smell you left behind in the toilet can cause violent headaches. Come on. Have another go. Believe me, you'll feel better afterwards. Starting now, you're going to drink two liters of water a day, and most importantly, no wine or beer. In the morning you are to have fruits, for lunch, *kwem* or *gwam*, and in the evening, *pèpèsoup*."

Bella heard about Clarisse's rather unorthodox methods, and scolded, saying, "We must earn our living, Clarisse. You know this as well as I do, so let's not chase the clients away."

Clarisse defended herself: "You haven't heard that people can die from an attack of methane gas? These people with unworthy digestive tracts aren't paying me enough for what I endure all day long. They should all be thanking me, these big whiners, or else they can take their smells somewhere else."

Clarisse toned things down, for a little while, but the situation worsened. The state of people's bellies seemed to be deteriorating with every passing day. She could no longer stand the stinking air. "And yet we're in the middle of an economic crisis," she thought. "Where are they getting these big paunches from? These people here have corrupted bellies." Her bottle of *Bien être* never left her. She was always on verge of asking them to use it as holy water—a small penance would do them more good than the diet she prescribed, she thought.

To keep Clarisse away from the toilet, Bella asked her if she wanted to be in charge of the herb and spice garden that Assumta had begun shortly before her death. "Everybody knows the feats of Clarisse's nose," Bella thought. "Why not entrust her with the task of internal cleansing?"

"Listen, Clarisse, instead of lecturing them, maybe you could make this *pèpèsoup* you're asking them to eat. Create health for their stomachs. You can use *bissap*, *pèbè*, *sèhè*, citronella, and all the herbs, all the little treasures that enlivened our grandmothers' dishes."

Warming to the topic, Bella continued, "Elsewhere, people have tea rituals. For us, it'll be a 'soup ritual,'" she said. "Everything will be prepared in front of the customers. They'll see everything. They must be assured."

Clarisse was delighted. She found Bella's idea very appealing and original.

"I'll start right away. It'll be big, this garden. You'll see what I will do in there. I can already see it in my mind. It will be a beautiful festival of colors and fragrances."

She stopped for an instant then continued, "But each ritual tasting will have to start with a walk through my garden. Customers will have to first nourish their eyes and hearts before they feed their bellies. They'll have to pay homage to nature before they can taste the soup."

Bella had not seen Clarisse this animated since she came to the Center. People weren't aware of her pretty dimples because she rarely smiled. Even though Clarisse was new to the Center, Bella knew her to be capable of deep resolve. Bella grew to admire Clarisse's calm but very confident air. Clarisse was unusually tall, and because of the quiet dignity that comes with suffering, she seemed to be gauging the world from the heights. Despite the gash that adorned her chin and her slightly detached left ear, Clarisse remained a very beautiful woman. She'd been found two years ago, half dead, in Paris's Bois de Boulogne. After a couple of months in intensive care, she was deported from France with several other undocumented aliens.

"And over in Sohok, at my paternal uncles', they all pretended they didn't know me!" Clarisse told Bella. "They forgot all the money I'd been sending for medicine, for my little brothers' food and lodging. And my uncle Etou, who was supposed to buy a plot of land for me, said that he hadn't received anything from me."

This was the only time Bella had seen Clarisse cry. Bella responded, "Clarisse—a mother never throws her child away. You came back to your maternal village. You're home here now. Be creative. Take initiative, and you'll survive, even if your cousin is no longer here."

Clarisse suggested to Bella an even more interesting idea for the toilets. She suggested putting up a sign on which the fees for each use would be posted. Then the only thing the person sitting under the flame tree would have to do would be to put the money into the cash box and help those unable to read. On a wooden sign that Clarisse spent weeks sanding and smoothing, she wrote down the following fees:

Moderate to tolerable smell . . . . 25 francs
Annoying, nearly noxious smell. . . . . 50 francs
Intolerable smell, nuclear-bomb style . . . . 100 francs
Restorative inhalation, whiff of *Bien être* . . . . 10 francs
Exclusive hand wash . . . . 15 francs
Washing *pula pula* (shared water) . . . . 5 francs
Beneficial hand balm . . . . 10 francs

Each customer, aware of the quality of effluvia that marked his visit, left the appropriate sum. To tell the truth, as a precaution, most customers paid the higher fee. Only those who merely urinated paid 25 francs. The shea butter balm was in such demand that Bella eventually asked one of her pharmacist friends to help her package it.

"That's a superb idea," Nobejo the pharmacist had replied. "No one is refining it right now. The butter will certainly bring me more than the glycerin and all the other oils we have had such a hard time selling. I could take care of it in the pharmacy, and of course we could set up a commission system."

She smiled indulgently, "That's not how I was seeing things exactly. We are paying you so you teach us the process of bottling and labeling, and we will do the bottling ourselves, here at the Center. Don't tell me you need to have graduated from pharmacy school to put shea butter in bottles. Our grandmothers have been doing it for years."

"Well then, why do you need me?" Nobejo replied, deeply stung.

"Because I want to learn how to get rid of the not always pleasant smell of crushed shea and palm. I want my shea butter to smell good. I also want it to be very beautiful. I want the bottle to have a pretty white label, the white of Khala-Kanti, with the following inscription: Beneficial balm, produced at the Good Hope Center. Natural ingredients: shea butter, palm butter, *okoumé* and ricinodendron essences."

"You're not going to ask me to bring my equipment here, are you?"

"If they're light, why not?" Bella said, with a smile she hoped was seductive.

Then she added, "Let's talk seriously. If we have to come to your place to do the bottling, then we'll give you a smaller percentage. I might eventually buy my own equipment."

The pharmacist made a quick mental calculation and understood that associating himself with Bella was in his best interest. Thus they quickly came to an agreement, and a few weeks later all the women in the region were fighting over the little jars of balm scented with local fruits and flowers.

Ironically, these were the same women who looked down upon the *Manyanga* and the *Kari* their grandmothers made. Some people attributed healing virtues to the balm, others found protective ones. Several women swore their rheumatism bothered them less since they'd begun using the balm. A young woman reported that, since using the balm, her husband came home every night. "What's more," she added with a knowing wink, lowering her voice, "when I put some on it, he is one hundred percent operational."

Some parents gave their children generous applications of the balm on the eve of exams. The famous Chinese Tiger Balm, or *small no be sick*, which they had all used before the Beneficial Hand Balm, was quickly replaced.

Yet Bella herself never attributed these virtues to her product. All that people could read on the back of the bottle was: "Your hands are the messengers of your soul, take care of them.

Beneficial Hand Balm."

But she didn't do anything to refute all that was being said about the products either. She let Street Radio take charge of advertising and cashed in on the results of this impromptu marketing campaign without protest.

Khasia often looked at her with a smile on his lips.

"I've never seen anyone like you!" he told her one evening when they were lying in bed. "When I was in Tingui, I would have so loved doing a profile on someone like you for my television newscast."

"One of nature's curiosities. That's right," said Bella, with feigned seriousness.

"No," replied Khasia, recognizing the self-derision that often characterized his lover's words. "No, I would most likely describe you as Zema, the goddess of harmony, the ancestor to the people of this region. She's the one who dried the disease-bearing swamps and turned this corner of the forest into a livable place. She could only be seen at the mysterious and serene hour of dusk, in the light infused with color that filtered through the leaves. Her body, whose contours were barely visible, drifted from house to house, leaving showers of shimmering music in her wake.

"She waged war against banality and everything that was ordinary. Every day, she gave each of her subjects a bowl of nectar that put them in a trance in which they were possessed with the desire to please, to seduce. Misunderstandings were solved. Everyone ate their fill and most importantly, people demonstrated unparalleled creativity. The village changed colors every week. Enigmatic motifs in ochre, yellow, orange, mauve, and white adorned the doors of the houses. The furrows in the fields formed beautiful crescent moons of rich soil. From small plots of land, men extracted enough to feed their families for several months. Even the women's calabashes were sharp and angular, and green palm wine flowed from iridescent palm trees."

Bella listened to Khasia, her gaze intense.

"You're telling me another of your stories, or else it's another of your poems," she said.

"No. Bella, if you'd grown up in Khala-Kanti, you'd have heard this story. That's where the name of our village comes from: Khala-Kanti, the spirit of music. Ask any old woman in the village. She'll tell you the story better than I can."

"So what made all this abundance disappear?" Bella asked.

"A few men in the village, we still don't know for what reason, decided one day to see Zema. They trapped her against a tree and undressed her. No one ever learned what they saw. They came back from it deaf and mute, and Zema disappeared forever. She may be drifting toward other more clement skies," Khasia added pensively.

"Watch out, then!" said Bella, laughing.

"Why do you think I treat you with such consideration?" he answered, also with a laugh.

Ever since Bella let her do as she pleased in her fields, Clarisse was beside herself with joy. She only dressed in green and golden brown, the colors of earth and plant life. She felt she was coming alive again. Dressing the part was her way of extending her mission into what she thought of as external purification. She remembered the woman selling African fabric in the market in Brussels, whose clothing was an indicator of her mood. Kiki was her name. She was the woman most reviled by the men in the African community of Molingo. She crisscrossed all the markets along the West African coast and came back with new fabrics decorated with new designs, to which the market women gave evocative names.

When Kiki wore her fabrics called "Capable Woman" or "Wealthy Woman," it was to remind the local gossip that business was going well. This also countered the rumors of bankruptcy that arose each time she traveled away from her shop. Then, according to her own close friends, when she suspected that her husband had dipped his cassava stick in the neighbor's soup, she broadcast her anger to the world, and above all, to the unscrupulous woman with a fabric named "I Run Faster Than My Rival" (a beautiful, predominantly green wrapper with a motif of two brown gazelles, one outpacing the other), or "If My Husband Goes Out, I Go Out" (a green, ochre, and brown wrapper with two birds in a cage, one of them about to leave). And when things had calmed down, she was likely to wear "My Rival's Envious Eye" (a wrapper whose central motif was a women's eye) or "My Husband Is Capable" (a rich white *bazin* fabric).

Clarisse met Kiki during one of her stays in Brussels. Her man at the time had taken her there to buy her a present. Clarisse had immediately been seduced by this strong, outgoing woman, who talked to two or three customers at a time while keeping a watchful eye on the cash register.

"You don't need to open your mouth for people to know what you're thinking. Let your clothes do the talking. Not just through the color. Let the designs come alive. They are what must convey the state of your soul to the world. My sister, your minis and your blouses are beautiful, but they are mute. For me, the language of my fabrics speaks louder than all the Street Radios in the world. I've also got wrappers that know how to lead to love and tenderness, wrappers that are more expressive than Wolof women's small white wrappers, or Baoulé women's *yéké yéké*. Look at this beautiful woman's arm stretching out affectionately toward this man's hand. Isn't that beautiful, eh? And these two birds with interlaced necks. In Brazza, people call this wrapper *bolingo*, it means "love." When a man comes in here to buy it, I know he's just met a new woman or he's trying to make peace with another."

Clarisse listened to all this attentively, emitting admiring noises.

"You're the Queen of the Wrapper," Clarisse told her.

Carried away, Kiki whispered to her, "You must come back to see me, I'll show you my exclusive collection. My suppliers didn't take me seriously before, but you know what? Now, they are using my patterns. But I don't say this to everybody," she continued, her voice even lower. "I am in the process of starting a sartorial revolution. You'll see, if God lets me live. I am in the process of devising an anti-mistress fabric for men's *boubous*. They put it on and there's no way they can look sideways, and even if they do look, there's no way they can function," she said, bursting with laughter.

Clarisse never returned to see Kiki in Brussels because her accident occurred a short time later. But in this corner of the forest, she found herself thinking about her and telling herself that someday she would find a way to get people to wear their emotions right on their bodies in order to find true symbiosis with their environment. Didn't the people of the southern forest once read the rhythms of their songs from the painted fabrics they wore? She told herself she would surely find a way to bring the plant-dyed and fiber garments back to life, belts made out of leaves, skirts of raffia, wrappers of beaten bark. But for the moment, with the help of two other women, she raked, she hoed, she dug, she marked the trail for the visitors. "It will be a pretty crescent with a hibiscus or daisy hedge," she encouraged herself.

Clarisse's garden became a focal point for the Center. She could boast about having welcomed, to her garden, all of the capital's high-ranking men who had gone there on a spiritual visit. She had eventually convinced Bella to let her have Assumta's large field. Bella hesitated because their friend was buried there. "Trust me," Clarisse plead. "Assumta is my sister, I'd be the last person ever to want to defile her grave."

The transformation this plot of land had undergone, in very little time, left everyone speechless. Clarisse spent every hour of the day in her garden. She created a tree-lined alley that she named the Nourishing Path. On either side of the path, she planted one of each of the species of trees that had been devastated by the truck drivers and their cronies. She took it upon herself to return to the forest the children who had been brutally torn from her arms. "I can hear her sobbing at night and my heart bleeds," she told Bella. "It's keeping me from sleeping." From the first morning light, Clarisse was in her sanctuary, putting this small corner of the universe back together with the relentlessness of a collector in a vandalized museum. Each *ayou*, each *azobé*, each *doussié*, each *sapelli*, had its double. She spoke their names with reverence, delighting as she stressed every one of their syllables: *acajou, iroko, ilomba, bubinga*. As Clarisse liked to explain to visitors during their Nourishing Walks, "It's a question of balance. Under this canopy, we are receiving the same amount of energy from each side of the pathway, our eyes are enjoying the same leafy feast. In their silent symphony, the trees are giving off energy that they toss to each other like a ball. The result of this constant back-and-forth envelops us, purifies us. Breathe," she continued. "Breathe in this plant fragrance, this protective perfume, and honor the earth of our forefathers. Speak the words she is waiting for. Speak the words she is begging to hear, 'Forest, I remember.' And may these words emanate from the deepest reaches of your soul."

And now these men, these big shots, who had taken part in the clearing of the forests and the abortion of cities, now these men were composing odes to nature, presenting their mea culpas to the trees, confiding their concerns to them, and entreating from them equanimity.

Clarisse had a few convenient benches installed and thus was born the Peaceful Nook where she completed her sermons, imploring each one to let the forest penetrate and awaken in them this primordial and perennial awe hidden within the empty carelessness of their daily lives.

"Let the forest murmur in your ears the keening of your ancestors' and your children's anxious despair."

In front of each tree was an inscription: *Kapokier*, support, buttress, pillow of the world; *Azobé*, tough, for its spirit of resistance, its indestructible frame; *Acajou*, subtle, for its finesse, its harmony with the colors of the earth; *Froufroutier*, regenerative, tree of a thousand virtues, the gods' gift to women; *Royal Ebony*, prince among princes, heart of the earth, color of the beginning; *Okoumé mentholé*, incense of the forest; *Padou mélodieux*, tree of a thousand sounds. Clarisse had spent hours composing these signs. She was proud of them. With these reflections, she sought to remind her clients about the cult their ancestors devoted to nature, a cult they had forgotten. She reminded them of the blasphemous acts they had committed against the forest, but most of all, of the place this forest deserved in the hearts of men.

"The trees in the forest aren't cruel, and whatever people tell you, men still lean against trees," she told them. "Let the trees support you, let your shadows intermingle."

Tears came to Clarisse's eyes every time she read these signs over again, especially at night, when you felt the breeze that met no resistance. By contrast, at dawn, when the sky shook itself from its cloak of clouds and the mist clung to distant treetops, the fine drops of dew on the tender leaves of her shrubs brought a smile back to her lips.

Her father's comments came back to her then. "He who follows an elephant's tracks will never become wet from the dew on the bushes," he often said. She, on the contrary, wanted to be the elephant, the usher guiding people toward her small world's peaceful, leafy sanctuary. She wanted this morning dew on her wrapper, she wanted to absorb it. "Dew is the sweat of the ancestors!" she often said.

In her view, during the night the ancestors protected the forest against the misfortune-bearing dream, and the dew was evidence of their work, of their visit. They'd washed the previous day's messy dust from the foliage so the vivid green of the leaves could feed people's eyes in the morning. The ones who succeed best are those who are the first to lay eyes on the damp leaves before the greedy sun quenches his thirst. "That's it," she told herself, smiling. "This is why the elephant is big, this is why it is strong. It absorbs the ancestors' sweat. It anoints itself with this celestial nectar."

At the far end of the field, Clarisse decided to set up a protective enclosure around her cousin's grave. She began with the most venerable of all trees, the tree that even young people, who were well practiced in modern forestry techniques, did not dare fell without the elders' permission and benediction. She planted the *essingang*, a *bubinga* that invited reserve. A mystical tree, the ancestors' cradle, it protected against the wrath of evil spirits. Then, in celebration of thwarted motherhoods the world over, she planted an *ilomba*, whose nourishing and salutary sap purified mothers' milk and neutralized all venomous bites. She also planted a *moabe* adorned with big, round fruits, vessels for a juice that chased death away. She winked at her childhood girlfriend when she planted side by side a light *bossé*, whose bark cured ailments said to affect the body's zones of love, and a *sangono*, a manly tonic, the nectar of studs.

Toward the middle of the field, she created a central place for the *tali*, tree of trance and audaciousness, and the *eboka*, whose drop of sap neutralized the impossibility of all illusions. To crown her kingdom, she planted the tree of truth at its entrance, a tree with red-orange flowers of which a single bud would extract secrets lodged in the deepest recesses of the soul. In front of Assumta's grave she planted the *wenge*, a beautiful ornamental tree with purple flowers that scourged itself twice a year, like the Khala-Kanti widows of old, to mark the destitution caused by a lover's death. She took great care of this tree, which mourned during the rainy season. She called it the tree of life and death. This was the tree that the most corrupt among her clients had to embrace endlessly.

Clarisse felt protected in this forest, her heart was set aglow, her soul unfurled. She swore that Assumta was now free from the sentence of the ancestors. She was everywhere, floating luminous in the shade of the arbor, nestled between the bright red heliconias and the dark amber stalks of the ginger.

Each species had its meaning and its place in the small botanical universe Clarisse had created. Each species governed the thousand contradictory expressions of the whole of mankind.

The Good Hope Center was buzzing with activity. The bar was never empty, and the drivers' old bedrooms were all occupied. Contrary to what people might have thought, city dwellers and their mistresses were not the only ones staying there. Top bureaucrats in search of spiritual protection now constituted the bulk of the clientele. These veterans of power who had become wealthy too quickly, these perpetual partiers were from time to time subject to crises of conscience. They slept badly, they told Bella and Clarisse. They all shared the same story. For some, this anxiety manifested itself in the form of nightmares.

Clarisse still remembered that a high dignitary had confided to her: "In my dream, I see myself on a beautiful red carpet. It's an official ceremony. I'm nearly by the side of the president, and just as I'm about to hold my hand out to him, someone pulls the rug and I take a tumble. I'm sure it's my assistant trying to outshine me in the boss's eyes."

"You have proof?" Clarisse asked.

"No, but I feel it."

"You're on good terms with the President?"

"Yes, I'm doing everything I believe he expects of me."

"How about what you should be doing?"

"In a certain manner, but that's less important."

"So why are you feeling unwell?"

"I don't know."

"You may be blaming yourself for something. We'll have to extend our walks on the Nourishing Path. Since you started on *pèpèsoup* and water, you've been doing better, but only the forest will be able to alleviate your conscience. When we're there, close your eyes and tell her everything that's weighing on your heart that you don't dare tell me. You must recover the lost unity between this world and yours. Tell the forest the hunter's prayer:

'*You, Nyama, master of everything, have pity on your poor son who has come to ask for your forgiveness. I have sullied your hands, the hands you gave me, when I killed another of your children. You know it wasn't my belly that guided my hand. I only wanted to feed the children you entrusted to me. I will not take part in this feast. I will not eat this meat. Do not punish me. Do not afflict misfortune on my household. My shot was skillful. I killed with respect, not insolence. I will celebrate its spirit for nine days and nine nights.*'"

These frequent contemplations eventually relieved the man's stress. He now seemed to be doing very well even if, in his view, the sole reasons for the disappearance of his nightmares were Bella and Clarisse's magical virtues. After many vain attempts, the two women realized that they would never be able to convince anyone that they had no supernatural powers.

During the following weeks, two of his friends came for a consultation. Seeing the sums that these well-to-do men were prepared to part with in order to protect their positions or even to be appointed to positions that they were coveting, Bella and Clarisse quickly understood that they could become the most renowned specialists in the region. For these important gentlemen who were beginning to visit the Center assiduously, Bella had set up a few rooms closer to Clarisse's garden so as to avoid indiscreet glances from clients in the bar. These big shots were served in their rooms and visits to the garden were so well coordinated that no two clients ever crossed paths.

These men needed to be heard, to be reassured, and that was what Bella and Clarisse did with skill and finesse. The men came back to unload their burdens, perhaps because they felt relieved to be in the company of ordinary women to whom they did not need to prove their masculine omnipotence. They talked, talked endlessly, while Clarisse and Bella listened. The two learned surprising, even stunning things, but Makang remained by far their most inventive client.

Makang showed up one evening, just before nightfall, wearing an overcoat with upturned collar, a great big hat, and dark sunglasses, like a detective in an old film noir. He asked his chauffeur to park far from the Center and walked the rest of the way. For a man of his importance, he stepped lightly. He moved forward with confidence, his eyes shining, even mischievous, looking less preoccupied than the usual clients did. Once he was settled in one of the bedrooms, he got rid of his outfit, and Bella and Clarisse were surprised to see the new General Secretary for Road Works, an illustrious son of Khala-Kanti. The only big shot from Khala-Kanti, now that Khasia had been demoted from this exclusive club—the very Makang who was responsible for the detour in the road that had transformed the village.

It had been a good long while since he'd last been seen in Khala-Kanti. He had come to the Center once, long ago, during Assumta's time. Ever since his mother's death, his visits to Khala-Kanti had become less frequent. He sent his chauffeur out to bring parcels to his old aunts on the occasion of funerals, baptisms, and the end of the year celebrations. As soon as he arrived, Clarisse sent for Bella. This man's inquisitive eye did not reassure her; he gave the impression he had something else in mind, other than discussing his contribution to the development of the village.

"I see the Center has evolved nicely," he said. "You must be turning an enormous profit here, between the bar, the small businesses, and your spiritual consultations."

Clarisse's heart sank. This man's self-confidence, his paternalistic tone, made her uncomfortable.

"Oh! General Secretary. Welcome home," Bella exclaimed.

"Not so loud, my dear. No one knows I'm here and I don't have time to stop by at my aunts'. I'm not staying very long. I was saying to your young colleague that you must be doing well here."

Bella did not answer. She knew several people were wondering whether she had the right to use Assumta's land. She also knew that Assumta's father was aware of the promise she'd made to his daughter. After a long silence, she said, "Things have changed quite a bit since Assumta's death, but her spirit surrounds us. She knew where this little center would go when she started. We're happy to be giving life to her vision."

Makang understood he was dealing with a substantial opponent.

"I'm happy to see my village develop. I hope you know that I have contributed to it myself in a rather important manner," he said.

Clarisse looked at him, stunned. She was wondering whether this man was talking about the same village that she was. Where is the water, the electricity, or even the paved road he had promised the villagers? Right away Bella realized that Clarisse would not hold back for long. She shot her a sharp look. Clarisse swallowed her anger. "Leave him to me for a consultation, and I will make him tremble," she said to herself.

"Listen, I am here because you hid something important from me. I, son of this village, I didn't know that the most effective seers in the country were here in my hometown," he said, a knowing look in his eyes. "It was one of your very important clients who told me about you. I helped his wife secure a big market, and he thanked me by sharing with me the secret of his meteoric rise. And apparently, you are its instigators."

The two women listened without uttering a word.

"I have heard the rumors of your prowess. I'm not going to beat around the bush. You know the time for appointments is coming up, and I think I'm going to be appointed Minister for Public Works. I've been consulting with a man from the north for a while. It's since I began working with him that I've been called back into the government. When I was relieved from my duties, everyone made fun of me. The friends who were practically living at my house all disappeared. You can imagine their surprise at my return," he added with a big burst of laughter, "and most of all the pleasure I take in giving them a hard time about it. In any case, what matters is that I can't consult with you personally. My sessions with this man in the north are costing me a fortune, but they've brought me very good results so far. In fact, I am in the middle of a treatment right now."

He stopped for a moment, and for the first time since he'd arrived, he seemed ill at ease, almost vulnerable, as if he were embarrassed, at a loss for words. Then he continued hesitantly, his voice lower, "But there's a small problem. I'll even admit it's a serious problem. My wife doesn't want to see this man anymore. I've threatened her. I've begged her. I've done everything, but she won't budge from her position. She refuses to see him and even refuses for him to live in our home like before. My seer told me that my wife's participation was essential to the success of the operation. He told me to be patient with her, but the political appointments are approaching and something must be done. So I would like to send my wife over to you so you can work with her. That is the goal of my visit today."

Bella, usually so quick to respond, was at a loss for words.

"But what exactly do you want us to do with her?"

Makang smiled and said, "You're pretty crafty, you two, and much too modest. I know what you're capable of. I'm not going to teach you how to do your work. She'll be here tomorrow."

With these words, he got up, pulled out a wad of banknotes from his pocket, placed it on the table, nodded to both women, and headed toward the door. Bella and Clarisse looked at each other, dumbfounded, and burst out laughing.

"You're the woman with a thousand ideas," Clarisse said, looking perplexed. "Tell me what we're going to do."

"We're going to treat her like a sister, like we treat every woman who comes to this center," said Bella with a wide smile that she hoped was reassuring.

The next morning, a black Mercedes parked in front of the Center. Véro, who was opening shop that morning, came down the steps to welcome the client. The chauffeur went around the car and opened the back door on the passenger side. No movement. He waited a while, leaned over, and spoke someone inside the car. Still, no movement. The little scene lasted a few minutes. Véro was observing all this from afar, not understanding what was happening. The chauffeur shut the back door and walked toward her, "It's my boss's wife. He was here yesterday, and he asked me to bring Madame to the Center. The problem is she won't get out."

"Wait here. I'll be right back," Vero answered.

Véro ran to get Clarisse and told her the story.

"Why don't you let her be? She'll come out of the car when she's ready," Clarisse answered with a shrug.

"But the boss is going to kill me if we go back to Tingui," interjected the chauffeur, who'd followed Véro.

"So what do you want us to do?" replied Clarisse sarcastically. "Haul her out of the car by force?"

The chauffeur didn't answer and went back to guard the vehicle. An hour later, a small woman, very pretty, and quite young, came out of the car. She was wearing a little straight navy blue dress and a pretty white headscarf. She was carrying a big tote and a blue-and-white-striped shawl was casually thrown over her shoulder. She headed toward the shop and asked for Bella. Véro led her into one of the bedrooms of the second building and asked her to settle in while she was getting Bella. Maléva waited for Véro's departure before she headed toward the center of the room. She examined its every nook and cranny to make sure there was no trap. Then, ignoring the comfortable wicker armchair and the bed, she took a straight chair that she pushed into the corner behind the door. She perched on the edge of her seat and waited nervously.

As usual, Clarisse was in her garden. This time around, she took her time before coming to talk to Maléva, hoping that Bella would come back, so she could avoid having to converse with the wife of a top bureaucrat who draped herself in her dignity.

When Clarisse finally pushed open the bedroom door, a little while later, she didn't see anyone, and just as she was about to close it again, she heard a tine voice say, "I'm here."

Clarisse came into the bedroom and said simply, "Hello, and welcome to our place."

The greeting the young woman gave in return was barely audible. She looked briefly at Clarisse and averted her gaze immediately. She held her tote tightly against her, like a schoolgirl about to have her book bag snatched away.

"My name is Clarisse. Bella is out. She'll be back shortly. Can we bring you something to drink?"

The young woman shook her head no.

"The punishment is over. You can leave your corner now," Clarisse said, laughing. "And watch out, next time you'll be kneeling."

The young woman smiled, recalling punishments meted out by the nuns at the College of the Assumption. Clarisse pulled a chair close to the young woman, who got up with a start and said in a firm tone that surprised Clarisse, "Above all, do not touch me."

Taken aback, Clarisse didn't know what to answer.

"I only wanted to come closer so that we could talk quietly. What are you so afraid of?"

Maléva didn't answer, so Clarisse decided to leave her alone until Bella came back. She got up, headed toward the door, then thought better of it and said, "Come with me. Come on, come."

The young woman continued to look at her with suspicion.

"I promise you nothing will happen to you. Come on. Come follow me."

Clarisse headed toward the garden with the young woman following her at a distance. Like a hunted animal, Maléva turned around repeatedly to make sure no one was following her.

After a few minutes, they reached Clarisse's tree-lined alley. Everything there was beautiful, organized with a precision that reminded her of the gardens she had visited with Makang during her notorious trip to France. For her part, Clarisse was already at the end of the path, which was about three hundred yards long. She was waiting patiently, observing the young woman's every gesture. She looks like a bird that's just been freed from its cage, she thought.

Maléva loosened her grip on the bag. Her breathing had slowed, but her heart was still pounding hard. She walked slowly, almost on tiptoe, like a hunter inspecting his surroundings. She stopped here and there to read the signs at the bottom of the trees. Reaching the end of the path, she let out a cry at the spectacle in front of her: the copper coloring of the leaves on the smaller trees, new shoots of the ground cover tinged with red, the golden green of dwarf palms, and here and there, pompoms of white and yellow flowers grouped in very dense bouquets.

"Oh my God. Where is this all coming from?" she exclaimed, eyes wide, hand covering her mouth.

"From my gut, from my soul, from my hands, like all our grandmothers' fields."

"No way! Who really did this? Would you look at these colors? It's so beautiful."

She headed toward the herb corner, where lovely mounds of citronella surrounded small furrows. In each furrow, Clarisse had planted different varieties of herbs.

"Oh, *massep*, I love this fragrance, and *maboda*. It's been a while since I last saw some," she marveled.

"It's beautiful, isn't it?" said a voice behind the young woman.

Maléva was startled. She hadn't heard Bella coming.

"I'm Bella. Sorry I wasn't here to welcome you. I wasn't expecting you so soon."

Maléva held her hand out to Bella, who smiled and said, "Unfortunately, I cannot shake your hand, but you can kiss me if you want."

Maléva stiffened again and told herself that, as a great priestess, Bella probably avoided shaking people's hands so as not to squander her energy. The long *boubous* Bella often wore revealed very little of her disability.

The three women headed toward the garden. Clarisse and Bella sat on the stone bench as Maléva, still standing, stared at them.

"Who are you? What exactly do you do in this little area, what is your specialty?"

"Mmm, let's see," said Bella. "We are women who live and work the earth, we keep this little Center and a little business, that's all. As for our specialty, it is us. We're trying to find ourselves again, we're simply trying to survive in a world that's very capricious at times."

"But why did my husband force me to come see you? What are you going to have me do?"

"Come, follow us," said Bella, walking toward the corner of the garden that led to the small clearing where Assumta was buried.

Shuddering, Maléva immediately thought about one of the *marabouts* her husband had taken her to consult, who had his clients touch a human skeleton. Clarisse and Bella prayed for a few moments in front of Assumta's grave, then turning to Maléva, Bella said, "We're here thanks to the generosity of the woman who is resting here."

Then the two women told Maléva how they had come to the Center, they talked about Assumta's expansive soul, her aspirations, and their daily lives.

Maléva was bewildered.

"But why did my husband tell me that you are very powerful seers? And he knows quite a lot about the subject, believe me! He's consulted the most famous *marabouts* in this country."

"People believe whatever they want, you know. It started like a game, and at first we found it amusing that people didn't believe us when we told them that our power was that of nature," said Clarisse. "You see, nature heals me. I hear the foliage whispering. I hear the silent melody of the butterflies and the dancing melody of the breeze. By these means, all my wounds are healed. And that's what I offer people who come here. We're all children of the forest, but we've forgotten how to communicate with her, how to love her, how to get her to heal us. We extract from her whatever we can, with arrogance, with contempt, and without gratitude. That's why we're doing so poorly in this country. That's why we're flat on our stomachs. The forest resents us, and as long as there's no harmony between her and us, the war will be endless."

Maléva was leaning against a tree and drinking in Clarisse's words.

"And all these people who come to see you go back home after understanding everything you just told me?"

"I don't know what they understand," Clarisse replied. "Never have we told them anything that is different from what you just heard. They seem to be more serene when they leave than when they first arrived. I think it's mostly due to the fact that we listen to them. The fact that they pour their hearts out certainly does them good."

Clarisse stopped for an instant, then added, "In the beginning, I think I scared them. Most of these people have no connection to the nature that's around them, and I was asking them to lovingly embrace trees and make peace with their consciences. Do you know who one of our most regular customers is?"

Maléva shook her head no.

"Well," Clarisse continued, "it's the Vice President of the General Council for Forestry Resources—you know, the one the forestry agents called Machete? He would like to be appointed President of the Council and doesn't understand why it's taking so long. I asked him to remember the number of trees he'd allowed his business friends to decimate. Then I asked him to compose an extended ode to the souls of the fallen trees, and ask each of them for their forgiveness. I told him this was the price he'd have to pay to find inner peace. I even added that if he didn't, he was risking death by a falling tree."

Bella opened her eyes wide and made as if she was lecturing Clarisse.

"How could you say such things to this poor man? Can you imagine his nights?" Then she added, with a half-smile, "Very ingenious indeed. Now I understand why he came here so often."

"For a forestry specialist, he didn't look in such good shape when he came here for the first time," remarked Clarisse, who was laughing as well. "His visits here can only have done him good. You're always telling me I'm going to chase customers away by talking to them frankly. So I did my best."

And in her turn Bella confided, "I asked one of our clients, a police captain called Cut-Head, on account of his meanness and unorthodox roughness with prisoners, to be kind and generous with one person each day. I prescribed this a little like alms are prescribed as a cure for greed or selfishness. I told him this would only be effective if it was a different person each day. The last time he visited, he told me he was sleeping better. Apparently people don't recognize him, they're wondering whether he's sick."

It was Clarisse's turn to look at her, stunned, "You too, Bella, you too?" And both of them burst out laughing.

Maléva's face had darkened. She seemed absorbed in her own world. After a moment, she asked the two women, "Does my husband know what you're doing here? I still can't understand why he insisted I come see you."

"He's your husband, you must know him well. He knows everything. He did all the talking the whole time; he even explained to us what we do," said Bella, laughing. "He got this information from a trusted source, of course. Then he told us you would be coming the next day."

Maléva had tears in her eyes.

"What he didn't explain to you was that I was in the car and refused to come out. For years he's been dragging me from *marabout* to *marabout*, from seer to seer, all for his damned appointments."

"Why did you come today, then?"

"So he would leave me alone," replied Maléva, "and also because I've had enough of him accusing me of being responsible for all of his professional troubles. Every day he reminds me that it's because of me that he wasn't appointed Secretary General a few years ago."

"Ah really? How is that? Is it true?"

"It's a long story, and to tell the truth, I don't know what to believe anymore. Five years ago, Makang was meant to take a trip to France. But what I didn't know was that he was planning to take one of his mistresses there. A girlfriend of mine who was a secretary at the Ministry of the Interior saw this girl's passport application, with Makang's name as guarantor. Of course, my girlfriend told me about it. I was furious. I get stuck with the work. I'm responsible for the children, for the family, and what does he do? He takes his mistress on vacation! So together, my girlfriend and I, we came up with a great plan. She got me an appointment with the National Security Director, to whom I explained that my husband wanted to abandon my three children and me to go to France to live with his mistress. A few days before his departure, my husband was called in to National Security, where he was more or less told that he would travel alone or with his wife. The ticket was paid. We left together, but throughout the trip he only talked to me when we were in public. When we came back, there was a round of appointments, but he didn't get any. A few months later, he was relieved from his duties. That's when the accusations started. I was the cause of his ruin, he would tell me daily. It was also at this point that he started consulting his seer in the North. That's where he's been dragging me these last two years."

Maléva stopped, wiped her eyes, and continued, "I have had enough. I've had enough of running to all these sellers of illusions, and I am especially fed up by the fact that a man of my husband's status could be so naive. This seer lived in our house for a year under the pretext of needing to purify its atmosphere each day. A scrounger, a pervert, that's who was living under my roof for a year. He was the one telling my husband when he should sleep with me—and that's not all."

Clarisse and Bella listened without making a sound. Nothing could stop Maléva. She was talking fast, like someone who had been denied the right to speak for a long time.

"You know why I came here? So I wouldn't have to go back to that crook. The first time Makang dragged me to this so-called healer, he made a circle of fire by planting about thirty fire sticks in the ground. Inside this circle there was another large fire, on which a pot full of herbs, leaves, and bark was boiling. The smell was so strong I almost fainted. He removed the pot from the fire and had Makang sit on a bench. He then asked him to breathe in the steam that was rising from the pot, with the request that he not open his eyes."

Then, imitating a northern accent, Maléva continued, "'Afterwards, you will rinse your face with a special water, a water that your wife, your partner in everything you do, will prepare for you.' I didn't understand what he meant and I was waiting quietly in my corner. Then he told my husband the sentences he had to utter every time he took a breath of this foul mixture. He then turned to me. I was only a few yards away from my husband. He asked me to take off my panties and squat above the basin of water placed right in front of me. I thought I was dreaming. I looked at Makang so he would say something, but he was too busy with his magic formulas. And this piece of garbage, this dog, was looking at me like a hyena that's just caught its prey. 'You want your husband to succeed, yes or no?' he asked me."

Maléva continued in a voice that was trembling with anger. "And without saying anything, my eyes turned toward my husband, I squatted over the little basin and the man knelt in front of me and began to wash my . . ."

She couldn't finish her sentence. She was shaken by sobs, as if she were reliving the scene. Clarisse had come next to her and was holding her tight against her bosom. Maléva blew her nose and continued, "Throughout this unspeakable washing, Makang was muttering incantations, and in the middle of all these formulas that I didn't understand, the seer was whispering, 'So, you like it? Does that feel good? You like it, don't you?' And my husband was there, just two steps away from me. It was as though he was selling me to the highest bidder, the most important thing being that he got his damned appointment. I never felt so dirty, so humiliated deep inside. Then later, with a knowing look toward me, this boor poured the water over Makang's head, while Makang continued to recite his magic formulas."

Bella wanted to ask her why she hadn't left, but she already knew the answer: leave to go where?

Maléva was visibly much younger than her husband. There must have been at least twenty years' difference between them. Despite her elegant air, there was something slightly unsure, indecisive about her, unlike her peers, the wives of high dignitaries, who wore the mark of their well-being on their foreheads, in their gazes, and most of all in their gaits. For her part, Maléva behaved as if the countryside of her youth had never left her. Bella understood that Maléva's story was the typical story of a girl from a family of modest means who marries a wealthy man. She also understood why Maléva could neither complain nor even leave her household. Without Maléva having to tell her, Bella knew what her family would have answered if she had dared confide in them: "Eat and keep quiet. He's helping your family. He's made you into a lady. Many young girls will fight to take your place." Bella thought back to her own life with Boualo and wondered why she didn't leave him either. The idea that a woman could have an honorable status without being under a man's tutelage was so strange to her at the time. And a mother's message was always the same: "Leave him to go where? What will your status be? Who will respect you?"

Maléva had calmed down. She'd picked up a little stick with which she drew circles in the gravel.

"That's why I didn't want to come. I didn't want to be fondled again; I didn't want to drink revolting potions anymore. I only wanted him to leave me alone. But I'm so happy that he dragged me here to you."

Thus began a strong friendship between Clarisse, Maléva, and Bella. Maléva spent one weekend per month with the women of the Center. As soon as she arrived, she would change her clothes and spend hours with Clarisse in her garden. Maléva returned from these visits more relaxed, more talkative. Even her appearance was becoming more youthful. Makang tried to probe to find out what was happening, but Maléva always answered with the most innocent air: "You know how these things are, it's like you with your *marabout*, I can't reveal what they are telling me, or what they are having me do, lest it ruin everything." Makang also felt like going to see the women of the Center, but was afraid of the consequences of a sudden break with his illustrious *marabout*.

The arrival of the executives from Disabled Without Borders set all tongues wagging in Khala-Kanti. For once, Street Radio found itself eclipsed. The organization's president, a young one-armed Frenchman, had succeeded in convincing the executives at Combined Media and the sponsors of the Afribroadcast satellite that had just been announced during the recent Franco-African summit in Montreal that broadcasting the satellite launch from the Good Hope Center of Khala-Kanti would constitute a great advertising coup. Africa was about to be thrust into the very heart of the technological era. All delays in development would be caught up.

Communications would speed up. Street Radio even announced that roads would no longer be necessary. There would no longer be a need to chase mice from the granary with broomsticks: now mice would be the carriers of electronic messages, the new sacred rodent. And so it was that, without clearly understanding how it had all come about, Bella found herself caught up in a media frenzy whose significance she could little imagine. This would be a first for the entire continent. The program would be broadcast in every country in Africa and throughout the world, she was told. All of Tingui's dignitaries were invited, and while happy that a project of such large scope took place in their country, they were furious that a diminutive woman from a remote corner of the country was the guest of honor.

A few months earlier, during the annual round up of monetary "adjustments" for those countries that had fallen off the path of development, some members of the World Bank had described Bella's operation as a model project. "Draw inspiration from her example," they told members of the government, while announcing a new structural adjustment plan. Addressing the Cabinet and businessmen in search of the ubiquitous model for economic recovery, the spokesperson for the World Bank had spent an hour outlining the brilliance of Bella's enterprise in paternalistic tones. "She successfully identified a need, a shortage. She used local resources. She transformed everything naturally in its place; she called in experts; she sought information about what was happening elsewhere in order to offer quality products to her clientele, and all of this was accompanied by a subtle and appropriate advertising campaign. Beyond that, she employed a marginalized population that would give pause to many other employers. For you see, she has understood that everybody likes things that are well made. She's understood that much, and this is why we find her approach interesting. To businesses like this one, businesses that value local natural and human resources, we are prepared to offer serious financing to help them in their plans for expansion."

The expert's preaching had cast a chill between Bella and some of her customers, which included many of the country's big shots, who tended to preach water and drink wine. They refrained from saying what they thought to the intrusive organization, which had its own motivations for supporting various policies and enterprises, and was also an expert in double standards.

Recalling from childhood nursery rhymes that the hand that gives is always on top, and also that the hand that awaits manna from heaven cannot menace, especially when it does not bear the mark of labor, all the big shots in Tingui had held back and followed the speech with pinched lips. Those who had been busy purifying themselves physically and spiritually at the Good Hope Center were astonished because they had neglected to notice how much the Center had grown, and because Bella's business sense had simply escaped them. They'd also failed to notice the expansion of the little craft market growing up next to the Center, which tourists visited daily. Bella had encouraged craftsmen to settle in the little community, while in return she charged a reasonable rent on the beautiful, elaborate stalls she had built, plus a small percentage of the profits. There were weavers, tailors, embroiderers, basket weavers, and potters, whose artistry showcased local talent. With her sisters' help, Bella had succeeded in creating what Tourism Ministries take years to realize.

During the official ceremony, Bella thanked the World Bank representatives for their laudatory words about her business. She praised the dedication and intelligence of the women around her, and most of all the precious help given by everyone she met. Deftly, Bella had managed to avoid compromising herself or attracting much glory to herself personally. She was suspicious of men who seemed in too great a hurry to use the Center as a new model for economic success. She also knew they would go back to their countries and she would find herself face to face with her customers once again, those influential men to whom she owed part of her success.

To the journalist who was asking her if she was happy that the World Bank was prepared to give her the funds necessary to grow her business, Bella replied, "We of the Center all appreciate the esteem that has been granted to us. But I must say I'd rather keep things as they are at the moment. Too rapid an expansion runs the risk of altering the Center's nature. However, we would like running water and electricity to be brought to our little village. I should say, rather, 'our little city' now. I also know that several women here today have ideas that have great merit. And of course," she added with an insistent look toward the high dignitaries, "government authorities must have much more important projects that may deserve more attention than our little Center."

Bella knew what impact she would have by raising the issue of water. Indeed, it was one of the simple projects the government could have taken on, especially on behalf of a productive little village like Khala-Kanti. Unfortunately, the funds of the National Society for Water and Electricity seemed intended for the maintenance of the installations in big cities, and of course, in these government functionaries' small villages. The World Bank expert turned toward the Minister for Land Use Planning. The minister knew what he had to do. In other words, if the government wanted to obtain the big loan from the World Bank, they would have to take the next obvious step necessary to get it.

Following the Afribroadcast satellite launch, Bella remained in the news, and journalists continued to film her little domain. Bella was glowing in her beautiful blue *boubou*. Her pretty, fine braids fell on her shoulders. "Here is our garden of aromatic and beneficial herbs."

Pointing with chin or foot, Bella was naming the plants and describing the mysteries of various trees. She gave the journalists a tour of the modest apartments, the workshops, the small bedrooms painted over for the occasion, the rooms where they welcomed their customers, and the renowned bar-restaurant, the heart of the entire operation. As she led the tour, she briefly told each girl's story and the circumstances of her arrival at the Center.

The woman journalist seemed deeply moved. She invited each woman to describe the role she played at the Center. Clarisse resisted. She saw this as exhibitionism, which she thought was exploitative. "So that's it," she told Bella, whom she'd taken aside. "You want me to tell them my life story, to offer myself up to these strangers so that later they can air all of this where they live, so people can despise us even more? Well, no! I don't want to be part of an international beggars' circle," she concluded resentfully.

Clarisse's words hurt Bella deeply.

"I know one thing, Clarisse: I'm trying to survive, that's all I'm trying to do. I am at war, and I use the weapons I can find, I don't have much choice and I make do as well as I can. Talk to them if you want, nobody's forcing you, but if you want to write your life, then speak loudly and clearly, otherwise people will do it for you."

Leaving Clarisse in her corner, Bella returned to her guests. She had become a professional in front of the camera, with an unshakable smile clinging to her lips and a serene air, when necessary. Her companions were seated in a half-circle around the journalist, who marveled at the respective stories of each of the women. At the end of the interview, the young journalist placed her microphone on her lap, scrutinized Bella's face, and asked, "What would you say to someone who wants to know who you are and what you do? What fight are you fighting?"

Someone burst out laughing from the other side of the room. The cameraman turned toward the corner where the laughter had originated. It was Clarisse, who had joined them but was sitting away from everyone else.

"Is this amusing? Tell me what you find amusing. I feel like laughing too, after everything I've heard," said the journalist.

"Yes, your questions are amusing," Clarisse retorted. "They're questions you ask when you have time, and especially when you have choice. Who are we? We are women, women who want to live, women who want to sleep in their beds at night, women who want to eat their fill. Women who want to do as they please. We are women at war," she concluded in a whisper, looking at Bella.

"At war against whom?" asked the journalist.

"We are at war against a world that leaves us few alternatives, and despite the disparity in weaponry, we have no intention of letting go."

"And what are your weapons?" the journalist asked.

"Anything that's available to us. Look around you, what do you see?" Bella interjected.

"The forest, trees," the journalist answered.

"These are our weapons, the trees and everything we find under their foliage. The earth is our weapon, desire our main artillery. On those days when we doubt, days when we want to leave everything behind, the temptation is to walk the old, known paths again. In these moments, this small corner of the earth represents the only buoy that keeps our fragile illusions afloat. Our fight is a fight for survival," she concluded pensively.

"Is this the only weapon available to women?"

"Everyone makes do with what they have," replied Clarisse. "Like our grandmothers and great-grandmothers, we are bound to the earth. They bequeathed it to us. Nothing has changed in the final analysis, you know! Even if we are deluding ourselves, we are still drawing from this nourishing earth in one way or another. We are a little more wounded than our grandmothers, and it is this that drives our fierce desire for survival. We are merely carrying on the task they began, although differently, perhaps exhausting ourselves a little less," she concluded.

An uncomfortable silence fell over the room. The camera lingered on each face, laying them bare one after the other. They all probed the lens, in return, with inquisitive and intrusive eyes. Some looked back fervently, others in confidence or audacity, still others with shivers of anxiety or desire. And as the camera lingered on Clarisse's face again, Bella's voice was heard in the background: "We are women whose fates are intermingled, bound by a past that's heavy with impossibility and a future set with jewels made of desires and dreams. We're no longer afraid of thunder and our feet have learned to land lightly on the moss and rocks of our forest paths."

From the far end of the room, Khasia was looking at Bella with pride. He was overwhelmed by the stories he already knew, but was listening to them as though hearing them for the first time. Like a teenager experiencing his first love, he felt like getting up and shouting to the room, "This is my Bella, my very own Bella!"

Listening to Clarisse, Bella, and the other girls talking about their lives and their aspirations had moved him deeply. He realized the extent to which he loved Bella. He loved her for what she was, for what she had become as the months went by, and he loved her most of all for what she had allowed him to become.

He was grateful to all these women who had come through the Center. Through his interactions with the women, he had learned to look more carefully at the small details of the world around him. As he had written to Joe, "My return to the village was not a flight, I now realize. I may have been unconsciously looking for a refuge, but I didn't go back to Khala-Kanti with my tail between my legs. I came here because it was the only safe place I knew, not like a cat coming back home to die, but rather needing to regain my momentum, and to redefine myself."

All of this seemed clear to him now. As a privileged witness to the lives of these courageous women who endured the worst abuse, he shed the encumbrances that defined his life. He had rediscovered the very essence of his convictions. Around Clarisse and her garden, around Bella, he understood he had come back to Khala-Kanti to get back in touch with what was truest in himself. He had come back to rid himself of the protective veneer that burdens us from our earliest years.

This ritual death of the old Khasia had given life to a Khasia who was prepared to own his fate. His students were the first to benefit. The readings for his classes were varied and complex, challenging the students in ways not experienced by other children in similar grade levels. The small school had acquired a garden as well, on whose progress Clarisse regularly came to check. Khasia lost neither his habitual biting humor nor his usual sarcasm, but the weight of the world no longer seemed to rest on his shoulders. He was willing to let life come to him, and his column chronicling Africa's rural world soon became a great success in *African Diasporas*, the monthly journal that Joe had recently begun to edit.

Bella and her companions were seated together around a plate of *koki*. They gathered in this manner on Sundays at lunchtime from time to time, on the beautiful veranda adorned with pink and orange-hued bougainvillea that Bella had set up behind their bedrooms. Life had resumed its daily pace after Disabled Without Borders' visit. The only thing that had changed was the more frequent visits from tourists who came to admire Clarisse's garden. Tékla, the woman who had given shelter to Assumta in Tingui, had arrived the day before, her eyes puffy, her face haggard. She had finally had the courage to leave the husband who tormented her and whose ultimate abject act had been, as she said with fire in her eyes, to impregnate her mentally retarded younger sister. There was little that surprised them anymore, and each one tried her best to be of comfort.

"Come on," said Clarisse. "Calm down. Eat!" she continued, rubbing Tékla's back.

"Listen. The newscast!" one of the girls said suddenly, and everyone stopped talking. Since Disabled Without Borders' visit, Bella had had a satellite dish installed, and the time of the newscast was now sacred. Frequently, armed with information from Street Radio and some of the occasional confidences revealed by their clients, the girls couldn't help but add further details to the journalist's remarks, or harshly tell him off for omitting certain facts. At that point they addressed the television set as if the person inside could hear them: "Who do they think we are? A hundred people died in this accident, not twenty. And everyone knows who's responsible, why are they claiming that the investigation is ongoing?"

Then came a sudden silence. Forks fell noisily. All of them had the wind knocked out of them. Only Bella kept eating.

"Madame Bella Mapék, founding director of the Good Hope Center, has been appointed Minister for Public Works and Land Use Planning by presidential decree."

"Bella, you hear, you hear that? They're talking about us! It's us, it's us!" Clarisse shouted, collapsing onto Bella.

All the women were up on their feet, people from the village were already running toward the Center.

"Say something. Speak, react," Clarisse told Bella, who still hadn't moved yet. "Did you know they were going to appoint you? Tell us, speak!"

"No, I didn't know anything about it," Bella replied eventually. Then she added, "I don't know what I'm going to do yet. There's the Center, you know."

But the end of her sentence was drowned out by joyful ululation. A party was improvised in the Center's bar.

"Are you happy?" Clarisse asked again. "We're at the top, we too have arrived, our ancestors haven't forgotten us," she added, tears in her eyes.

Everyone accepted this appointment as if fate had imposed it. Only Bella appeared not to understand what had just happened to her. A frozen smile on her lips, she didn't quite know how to react. She couldn't help thinking this was a poisoned gift. "They're trying to unwind me like an old braid," she thought. "Someone forced their hand. I'm sure someone forced their hand, it's incomprehensible."

Thunder raged in her head. Between the racket caused by the people who were dancing and the torrent of ideas swirling in her brain, she felt her head was going to explode. She regretted the loss of her hands, which she would have liked to press against her ears to silence all this noise, or better yet, press against her temples to alleviate their pounding pain.

She came down the steps of the veranda, her gait uncertain, almost staggering, and headed toward the hedged alley of Clarisse's garden. The songs of the birds, the rustling of the leaves, all these small, daily noises that anchored her to this village, comforted her. She crossed the flower garden, then the herb garden, and headed toward Assumta's grave. She had developed the habit of seeking rejuvenation near her old friend.

The soothing atmosphere of this lush green garden always managed to calm her. She sat down, closed her eyes, and saw herself drawing small, interlaced circles in the dirt. She was playing with freshly turned earth, earth that contained her friend, earth that had become her friend. Assumta held her hand out to her, a hand from beyond that carried life and death, a hand at once palpable and invisible, fraternal and deadly.

Bella shrugged as if to say, "But you should know I can't hold my hand out to you." Then she answered her friend's gesture with a smile. In turn, Assumta addressed to her an enchanting, reassuring, and knowing smile that said, "I understand. I had forgotten." And so Bella continued, "My sister, my daughter, my friend, you of the caste of the immortals, sing my lineage for me, find the signs of my future in the cowries' source, explain to me the meanderings of my life. You used to tell me that I would go far. I thought you were talking about the Center. But you heard the joke they played on me at lunchtime. It's over, it's a trap; they're waiting for me to trip over it, so they can knock me down. They think I criticized them in front of the whole world when the satellite was launched. They're accusing me of lacking in deference too. Yet I was careful about what I said, I weighed every one of my words, Khasia had warned me."

"It's true, I'd warned you. So, are you going to accept this appointment or not?"

Bella let out a strident cry and leapt to her feet. She landed in Khasia's arms, he was laughing.

"Oh my God, you scared me," she gasped.

"Scared you? But you asked a question," Khasia answered, his eyes shining. "You are scared, you, the steadfast Venus? You're scared of a small administrative position, you're scared of showing them that you could run a ministry with ease?"

"That's not exactly it. How many times did you tell me yourself that Tingui was a steamroller? That people with the best intentions in the world were turned into puppets in a matter of months? That's the disease I'm scared of. I'm scared I'll have my hands tied," she said.

Khasia drew close to her, took her face in his hands, and asked her softly, "Which hands are they going to be tying up, my Venus? Show me the hands they're going to tie up!"

Bella looked at him, stunned.

"You're the woman of a thousand ways," he continued. "You're like your namesake of the forest, Kul Mapek. You cannot be caught, don't ever forget it."

Khasia didn't sleep all night. He couldn't understand what was happening. Bella's entire body was shaking, she had awakened screaming. Her body seemed to be in the grip of an epileptic fit. Khasia had to lie across her in order to calm her disjointed movement. When she came to, she curled up on the bed and started sobbing.

Khasia was becoming alarmed. For a few moments he'd thought it was a nightmare, but now he was wondering whether or not she was seriously ill.

"What is it? What's wrong with you? Should I take you to the hospital?" he said.

"No, to the water, to the water," she gasped.

"You want some water?"

"No, I want to go to the water."

Khasia didn't understand.

"Take me to the water," she yelled. "Take me to Maéba."

"To Maéba? Maéba as in Maéba on the ocean?"

Bella nodded yes.

"Are you sure? It's three hours away, you know?"

"Take me to Maéba, I need to wash myself," she insisted.

Khasia no longer knew what to say, he didn't even dare ask her why Maéba and not the stream in Tikikoum, which was about six miles away.

"Ok. I'll start the car and then come get you," he said, caressing her shoulder lightly.

"No, I want to walk," she said.

Khasia looked at her, dumbfounded.

"But it's at least ninety-three miles away, you know that well."

"I want to walk, I need to walk," she sobbed.

Khasia understood that something troubling was happening within this woman, who was usually so measured. He went and awakened Clarisse and explained what had just happened.

"Follow us in the car. I hope to convince her to get in the car later on."

Bella and Khasia disappeared in the night mist, she in front, he behind, and about a hundred yards behind them, Clarisse in the small Suzuki with only the sidelights on. About a mile down the road, Khasia eventually convinced Bella to get into the car. He whispered a few words to Clarisse, who yielded the wheel. They helped Bella settle in the front seat. Clarisse took Bella's face between her hands, pressed it against hers, then closed the door and watched the small car drive away.

When they reached the beach at Maéba, Khasia opened the car door and helped Bella out. She immediately took off her shoes and walked toward a dune, which she climbed with the agility of someone who was used to doing so. Khasia was following her with difficulty. He still couldn't understand what was happening.

How could Bella have known this place? In the distance a few canoes and casting fishermen were visible. Bella was radiant, like an apparition, the wind caused her beautiful white *boubou* to swell and her long braids floated on her shoulders. Her eyes closed, but her head turned toward the sky, absorbing the sun's rays. She came down the ocean side of the dune, undressed and bare-chested, her small white wrapper around her waist. She headed toward Khasia, collapsing on his chest. He held her very tightly in his arms. They let themselves flop onto the sand. Something had just been confirmed in this embrace, but he didn't know what.

After a long while, Bella got up, and without saying a word, walked toward the sea. Khasia was stunned. Somewhere deep inside, a voice instructed him to stop her, to reassure her, to tell her how beautiful, strong, desired, loved she was, but something even stronger kept him from doing so. He let her be, he watched her as she moved farther away, absorbing every one of her silent gestures. Behind her, he was shaking, his fingers stiff, his brow sweaty despite the ocean breezes.

Bella glided forward to the water with grace. It looked as if she were floating. Not once did she turn back. The water was nearly up to her shoulders, but Khasia could have sworn that she was not swimming, that she was still walking on water. He drew close to the sea, so as not to lose sight of her head. With each step he took, the sand gave way under his feet, disorienting him. He missed the steady firmness of the forest's sponge-like soils.

He knew how to decipher the language of brambles, of twigs and bushes. The small animals he hunted in his childhood had innocently revealed to him the secrets of the tunnels they crisscrossed, and even the shadows of the big trees that sheltered him had revealed their mysteries for him. But the sea, this undulating blue-tinged mass, this strange and unknown thing, was indifferent to his call. When the distant dot that Bella had become disappeared, he fell to his knees and sobbed like an orphan.

As the sea remained silent to his call, Khasia headed back toward the dune. Haggard, he stared at the sand, wondering what had just taken place and how he would explain it to the others. They'll all say I sold her to the water fairy so I can get my position back. No one will ever believe that I let her do it. And why in God's name did I let her do it? Why? For a long time, his fingers traced signs in the sand. Without realizing it, he created a complex geometric design whose center looked like the game of *atéké*. In each square, he placed cowries and small shells his fingers had randomly dug out while he drew. In this silent exchange with the goddess of the sand, he gave her back her subjects, hoping she would give him back his Venus. Didn't his father tell him that the person who received cowries in an exchange could be struck by immediate death, condemned to permanent silence for refusing these pearls from the gods, the very symbol of the word?

As evening began to fall, exhausted, disoriented, Khasia decided to go to the closest dwellings to see whether the fishermen would help him search for Bella. When the last canoe abandoned the futile quest, Khasia remained alone on the beach, his gaze empty, wandering like the spirits whose souls *Mami Wata* had imprisoned.

When he came back to the car the following morning, Bella was there, leaning against the door.

"But, but, but…" said Khasia, who nearly fell over backward.

"Yes, I know. I know you were worried. I am a daughter of the ocean. My village is about six miles from here. I spent my entire childhood on this beach. I know its every nook by heart."

"I. . . I thought…" Khasia was crying hot tears, his voice choked.

Bella pressed her face against her lover's mouth.

"I know what you thought, but the sea decided otherwise. I am her daughter. Whatever I do, she watches over me. It is time I tell you the details of my birth. I was born in the water. My mother, who was more than eight months pregnant, fainted at this very spot and the sea's waves pulled me from her womb and carried me, rocked me, until people came! No one has ever known how long the two of us floated."

Khasia was still looking at her with an incredulous look on his face. It seemed that even her voice had changed. There was something light in her tone. The rhythm of her words echoed her undulating gait on the sea. Khasia held her very tightly against him. "You are my mermaid of the waters," he whispered. Her only answer was, "You must help me find my daughter."

Khasia wasn't asking questions anymore. He understood that Bella would reveal herself in her own time.

"Do I make a left or a right?" was all he asked once she'd settled in the car.

"As you wish, the two roads cross a bit farther on," she replied. Then she closed her eyes to better enjoy the sounds of the sea.

"What is your daughter's name?" Khasia whispered.

"Mialo ma Ilali, which means: 'As you wait for happiness, be as hard and strong as a stone.'"

AUTHOR

Angèle Kingué is Professor of French and Francophone Studies at Bucknell University. She is widely recognized for her work on the teaching of Francophone African Culture and Literature. An accomplished author, she has published two novels, *Pour que ton ombre murmure encore* (Paris: L'Harmattan, 1999) and *Venus de Khalakanti* (Bordeaux: Ana Editions, 2005); two adolescent short stories, "Echos d'enfance" (Ville LaSalle, Québec: Hurtubise, 1993) and "Une voix dans la nuit" (Montréal, Québec: Hurtubise, 1998); and a children's story published in five languages, "Qui est dans la lune?" (Paris: L'Harmattan, 2005). Many of her short stories have been reprinted in popular French language textbooks and have been the subject of academic analysis. Angèle Kingué earned her bachelor's degree in bilingual studies at the University of Yaoundé, Cameroun, her Master's degree in Applied Linguistics and Teaching English as a Second Language at the University of North Wales in Bangor, Great Britain, and her Ph.D. in French and Pedagogy at the Pennsylvania State University.

TRANSLATOR

A writer, editor, and translator based in Brooklyn, **Christine Schwartz Hartley** has translated *Commentary* by Marcelle Sauvageot (New York: Ugly Duckling Presse, 2013); *African Psycho*, by Alain Mabanckou (New York: Soft Skull Press, 2007); and *Kate Moss: The Making of An Icon*, by Christian Salmon, and *Mamika: My Mighty Little Grandmother*, by Sacha Goldberger (both New York: HarperCollins, 2012). A former deputy editor of *Art + Auction* magazine and contributor to *The New York Times Book Review*, *Bookforum*, *Interior Design*, and *Elle Decor*, among other publications, Christine Schwartz Hartley is also responsible for the 2010 reissue of *Spécialités de la Maison*, a compendium of recipes contributed by early 20th-century celebrities and socialites. French-born, she holds a diploma from the Institut d'Etudes Politiques de Paris, a Master's in journalism from New York University, and a licence ès lettres (English) from the Université de Paris IV-Sorbonne.